THE HOME BOOK OF
GREEK COOKERY

*For when you write a book on
Cookery, it will not do to say:
'As I was just now saying';
for this Art has no fix'd guide
but opportunity, and must
itself its only mistress be.*

Athenaeus
The Banquet of the Learned
or
The Deipnosophists

The Home Book of Greek Cookery

*A Selection of Traditional
Greek Recipes*

by

JOYCE M. STUBBS

FABER AND FABER
24 Russell Square
London

First published in mcmlxiii
by Faber and Faber Limited
24 Russell Square London W.C.1
Printed in Great Britain by
Latimer Trend & Co Ltd Plymouth

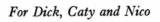

For Dick, Caty and Nico

ACKNOWLEDGEMENTS

This book would have been impossible to produce without the help of Lena Triantaphyllidou, George Begley, Crisulla Tombaziadi and the many cooks, professional and amateur, often in remote parts of the mainland and the islands of Greece who have readily given up to me the secrets of their favourite dishes. To them all I offer my grateful thanks.

9

CONTENTS

FOREWORD

No exaggerated claims ought to be made for the Greek cuisine. It is limited in range and (being based on oil rather than butter) is generally more savoury than subtle. The best things to eat in Greece are the simple things—grilled fish, and meat roasted on the spit—which are to be found all over the world. Nevertheless, there are characteristically Greek dishes that can be very good indeed, when they are well prepared, and most of them are here, in Mrs. Stubbs's book.

Many people who have travelled in Greece have had little or no experience of Greek cookery at its best. This is not a country of restaurants; most people go home to eat in the long afternoon interval from work, and make a light and informal meal late in the evening from what remains from midday. The standards of home cookery (often excellent) are not maintained by critical customers and restaurants and *tavernas* seldom have to cater for people who (in Henry James's phrase) 'thoroughly know and care'.

Mrs. Stubbs thoroughly knows and cares, and she is doing a real service in recording for those who know them (and introducing to those who do not) such delicate and exquisite things as aubergine salad, artichokes à la polita, fish à la Spetsiota and the fricassee of lamb and lettuce, and also such succulent ragouts as the styphadho. They are a genuine contribution to European gastronomy.

ROBERT LIDDELL

INTRODUCTION

Ye have the Pyrrhic dances yet
Where is the classic cooking gone?

After Byron

The great romantic poet in one of his earthier moments might well put this question on a superficial acquaintance with Greek food. The best of Greek food is not easily found by the casual visitor. The French who freely admit that they are leaders of the world's culture rightly consider cooking one of the greatest of their arts. Italian cities eagerly claim certain dishes and styles of cooking as their own: Milanese, Bolognese. Yet Greece was far more civilized, far sooner than any other Mediterranean country. Among its other triumphs, what of its cooking? And what of its cooking today? To answer the latter question is the purpose of this book. For there is a distinct identity of Greek cooking which is enjoyable in itself, enjoyable for its difference, and which traces many of its origins from the magnificent past.

In his book *Athens and the Greek Miracle*, the late C. P. Rodocanachi, himself a Greek, sheds a particularly Attic light on the achievements of his countrymen. 'What happened in Athens in the fifth century B.C. is so unique in history that it has been called the "Greek Miracle". These words are intended to express the prodigious crystallization within a bare hundred years and in a small country, of every perfection in art, in thought, and in social organization.' No mention of cooking you notice. Yet the Greeks of those days were not an austere people whose main relaxation was arguing with Socrates. Indeed Alcibiades, a particular friend of Socrates, was such a man for a party that it brought him into trouble with the law.

Alcibiades may have been an irresponsible young man but no one could say that about Plato. It is a pleasure to recall Plato's reply to a question put to him under an olive tree which may well be the same one which still grows near the Athens fruit market today.

'What are you reading?' he was asked. The sage, indeed, was not mulling over the Socratic dialogues or a definitive work on the City State. He was studying the latest Philoxenus on cooking. Warming with the enthusiasm due to a serious subject Plato began reading extracts of special significance—considered opinions on which fish should be baked and which would be better boiled; practical advice, such as the need to beat octopus until tender and that large ones are better boiled, though his personal preference is for two smaller ones baked. Red mullet, says Philoxenus, are not of much account—and I agree with him—though they are accounted a great delicacy in modern Greece and are priced by the kilo on restaurant menus—presumably to avoid startling the customer when he gets the bill.

Philoxenus had one achievement for which he should be living at this hour. He persuaded Greek cooks to serve food very hot. I remember once in a restaurant in Athens sending a steak back because it was served on a cold plate. When I explained to the waiter that hot food should be served on hot plates he looked at me like a reasonable man presented with an unheard-of suggestion and said: 'But it is summer.'

Greek cooking is often irresponsibly dismissed as being derived from Turkish and Italian sources without any character of its own. But historically the facts are the other way round. It is true that most Greek dishes today have a Turkish name but this is hardly surprising when one remembers that Greece was occupied by the Turks for nearly four hundred

Introduction

years. After the fall of Constantinople in 1453 until the liberation of Greece in 1830, Greek cooks were compelled to refer to their dishes in the Turkish language. The mere fact that they acquired Turkish names led to the belief that the dishes themselves were of Turkish origin. Although the history books do not mention it this seems a good ancillary reason for throwing off the yoke of the oppressor.

It was indeed from the fifth century B.C.—the century of the 'Greek Miracle'—that the culture of the Greek cuisine began to spread through the Mediterranean from Lydia to Sicily. It was through the Greeks that the Romans improved their cultural and gastronomical standards by employing Greek tutors for their children and Greek cooks in the kitchen. Lucullus, whose name has become an adjective for gracious eating as well as the name of expensive restaurants everywhere, founded his reputation on Greek cooking.

Although the ancient Greeks were noted for their simplicity of living they recognized the standard of cooking among the arts—they acknowledged Thimbron the Athenian as surpassing all cooks in skill and genius—'genius' you note—the word that book reviewers today claim they never use lightly.

The intimate relationship between civilization and cooking was argued with clarity and enthusiasm by Athenaeus who lived over the latter part of the second century A.D. into the third century. He himself was a native of Naucratis in Egypt, resident in Rome and in his famous book the Deipnosophists or *Banquet of the Learned*, he described many methods of cooking and serving food as used in Greece today; notably the strewing of herbs on fish or grilled meats and sauce boats full of oil and vinegar. Even *keftethes* the popular meat balls of Greece today are honourably mentioned by him.

In the Middle Ages many cooks found their way into the Orthodox monasteries where they provided succulent dishes for the appreciative monks. To distinguish them in their work they wore tall white hats instead of the black ones of the regular monks and this tradition of a chef's cap is universally preserved today.

Introduction

Where now is the food that inherits the glorious tradition? It should not be judged by the meals offered to tourists and travellers in *tavernas*, second class hotels, first class hotels and luxury hotels. There are exceptions where the food is both Greek and wonderful—alas, very few and far between. But the luxury hotels play safe for an international clientele—the food is international and reminds you of the Midland Hotel, Manchester, or the Hassler in Rome. In the *tavernas* the execution is often crude and for the Greek who visits a fashionable *taverna*, food is not the first object. He goes to enjoy an evening out with his family and friends; to hear popular music; to see a floor show and regardless of expense to be seen. On these occasions he patronizes establishments serving so-called Continental food. This is thought to be more *chic* and as the party probably has little acquaintance with 'Continental' food there is a lack of standards by which to complain. It is very rare to find cooking in the true Greek manner at such a *taverna* and the result is a meal lacking in character and one which lowers the spirits.

But this is all on the surface. The long tradition of fine cooking still exists in Greece. And although the casual visitor may not always discover them a full range of excellent and truly Greek dishes can be found. There are cooks rich in knowledge and enthusiasm. I have been so lucky as to meet many of them and talk with them, often in their own kitchens at home or in *tavernas*. Many of these recipes have been found in remote and unfrequented parts of the mainland and the islands, and they are a selection of the best that I have found in Greece over the last ten years.

I have been fortunate beyond reasonable expectation in my friendship with one naturally gifted and dedicated to cooking; one to whom the tradition of Greek cooking has been handed down as poetry and music were handed down among the bards—Crisulla Tombaziadi.

Talking Under the Pine Tree

For several years my family and I have spent our summers

Introduction

on the island of Spetsai in the Cyclades. Spetsai is not far from Athens. It is beautiful and progress has not yet overwhelmed it. Our house has been an olive estate, one of the loveliest in the Mediterranean. There I learnt many of the most valuable secrets of Greek cooking—unpublished and preserved only among friends and families. It was Crisulla who taught them to me. Not only has she taught me much of the art of Greek cooking but some of my happiest memories of those wonderful months are of sitting under the great pine tree talking of food with Crisulla.

Crisulla's love of food and cooking is probably hereditary. Her father and her grandfather, both Greek Orthodox priests, were gastronomic heroes who still live in the folklore of the island. It is related that on one occasion her father was fasting and could eat neither flesh nor fowl. Friends, undoubtedly instigated by the devil, assailed him with temptations to help himself from a dish of delicious roast quail. The priest was a man not only of piety but of resource. Making the sign of the cross over the dish of quail he said: 'I bless these aubergines,' and smartly popped a bird into his mouth.

Crisulla combines this resource with an intense interest and talent for cooking. With a few vegetables she can make a dish which is exciting and delicious by the addition of aromatic herbs from the hillsides; all that comes fresh from the sea, no matter how unpromising will be transformed by her into a delicacy. And with her native islander's knowledge whenever she takes a walk she brings some treasure to eat—an apronful of wild figs or sea urchins prickly without, succulent within.

It was fitting that our talks should have taken place on Spetsai, most Greek of islands, in the setting of the tall cypresses and aromatic pines surrounding the house, and of the silvery olive trees billowing down to the sparkling Aegean before and away to the dark mountain behind. The full subtlety of Greek cooking makes itself felt among the sturdy olives that have provided so much towards the preparation of the food, and there is a blending of the senses when one dines with the sweet aroma of the pale blue wisp from the olive-wood fire in the kitchen.

It is said that man can live off these amazing olive trees. When the heavy winter rains strive to wash the soil from the rocky land out to sea it is the olive trees that hold it so that wheat and vegetables can thrive to provide food for man and animal.

Preserved in brine and their own oil the berries, black and shiny as the eyes of the women who gather them, form with bread and goats'-milk cheese the basic sustenance of the working people.

Crushed, the berries give oil which, in its refined form, is the universal remedy for ailments from gripes in the cradle to the afflictions of failing old age. The oil of the olives is both a food and a cooking medium of unequalled nutritive value. Modern dieticians are taking note of the comparative absence of heart troubles in countries where the oil of the olive tree takes the place of animal fats in the diet of the population.

Not a particle of the product of the olive is without its value. The residue of the oil is boiled down for soap and the remaining pith and pulp returns to the land as fertilizer or is used as fuel for the domestic fire or industrial furnace.

The services of the olive tree to man do not end with its fruit and the oil it produces. Throughout its centuries of existence—as we have seen there is a tree in Athens under which Plato is reputed to have sat—the annual pruning provides fodder and bedding for sheep and goats; the hard, close-grained timber from the heavier branches is material for dwellings, furniture, tools and utensils; and the withered or waste wood provides winter warmth for the hearth and fuel for cooking throughout the year.

The ancient Greeks well knew their indebtedness to the olive and taught its uses to the less advanced races of the Mediterranean. The cradle of modern civilization was also the cradle of Mediterranean cooking as it is practised now. In Greece today there is a long-established cuisine which is originally and truly Greek. An antiquarian interest does not

Introduction

necessarily imply enjoyable food but the Greek kitchen offers many exciting dishes which can be enjoyed by everyone including the gourmets of international standing. Yet the essence of Greek cooking is informality.

All the ingredients needed for the following recipes can be obtained in England. Perhaps a total diet of Greek dishes out of their own setting and climate would pall in the cold Northern countries. But for the family looking for a change; for a friendly lunch or supper party with a difference; for those who simply like good food or have the enterprise to try something new, a Greek meal is as refreshing as a day in the sun. To those who have known Greece it will bring back nostalgic memories, to those who have yet to visit the Hellenic world it will give an indication that there are pleasures other than those of scholarship and scenery to come.

One of the world's earliest cookery books was the work of Archestratus republished under such titles as *Gastronomy*, *Dainty Dishes*, etc. So commanding was his authority that he became known as the Hesiod of Epicures.

Now Hesiod, as I need scarcely remind my readers, was a poet said to have flourished in the time of Homer. To refresh the memory of those who have not their Lemprière's Classical Dictionary at hand: 'The Greeks were so partial to the poetry and moral instructions of Hesiod that they ordered their children to learn all by heart.' A powerful recommendation for a cookery book this, but then where did the word epicure come from but from Greece. Webster's Dictionary with a cautious warning that this was not really what Epicurus the master meant, defines 'Epicure' as 'one devoted to dainty or luxurious sensual enjoyments esp. to the luxuries of the table'. As this defines the purpose of cookery books rather more clearly than it is usually expressed, I hope that you will find some of the dishes in this book equal to such a high standard.

A NOTE ON GREEK COOKING

When I first began to write this book, Greece had not yet come into line with the majority of countries using the weights and measures of kilos and litres. They used a measure known throughout the Middle East as *oka* and *dramia* for both solids and liquids. Despite the introduction some years ago of kilos and litres as the official weight and liquid measures, many people, particularly country folk, still think in terms of the old *oka*. Since Great Britain is to change to the metric system I have given an approximate table of weights and measures to assist cooks who, like myself, become confused and bewildered when faced with a recipe given in a different measure from the one with which they are familiar.

Personally, I find the American practice of measuring in cups most practical, for whatever the most ill-equipped kitchen has not, it surely will have a cup!

Greek cooking is all done very much by rule of thumb and scales, apart from checking the vendor, are rarely used in the kitchen. A handful of rice, a cup of this, a glass of that; much is left to the ingenuity of the cook who has a feeling for food. The Greeks being the complete individualists they are can never do anything the same way twice nor can they agree among themselves on a correct method of procedure. This makes it very difficult to give exact amounts of everything in a book on Greek food and I strongly advise anyone following a recipe for the first time to taste frequently, particularly when using herbs, lemon juice or olive oil. Where possible, the amounts in the following recipes have been

23

given in pints, pounds and ounces and should serve four to six people.

Every cook should know the vagaries of his or her own oven, whether it be fired by gas, electricity, hard fuel, wood or paraffin. Therefore, I have not given any temperatures for oven cooking, assuming that any cook will know what is meant by a hot, moderate or cool oven.

WEIGHTS AND MEASURES

1 kilogram = 1,000 grams = 2·2045 pounds
1 lb. = 16 oz. = 453·582 grams or roughly 450 grams
1 oz. = 28·3495 grams or roughly 30 grams

Grams	Oz.		Grams	Oz.
15 =	$\frac{1}{2}$		200 =	7
20 =	$\frac{2}{3}$		225 =	8 ($\frac{1}{2}$ lb.)
30 =	1	($\frac{1}{4}$ kilo) 250 =	9
50 =	$1\frac{2}{3}$		285 =	10
60 =	2		300 =	$10\frac{1}{2}$
80 =	$2\frac{2}{3}$		320 =	$11\frac{1}{3}$
85 =	$2\frac{3}{4}$		400 =	$14\frac{1}{4}$
90 =	3		450 =	16 (1 lb.)
95 =	$3\frac{1}{4}$	($\frac{1}{2}$ kilo) 500 =	18
100 =	$3\frac{1}{2}$		600 =	21
113 =	4		640 =	$22\frac{1}{2}$
125 =	$4\frac{1}{3}$		675 =	$1\frac{1}{2}$ lb.
140 =	5	($\frac{3}{4}$ kilo) 750 =	1 lb. 10 oz.
150 =	$5\frac{1}{3}$		900 =	2 lb.
160 =	$5\frac{2}{3}$		1 kilo =	2 lb. 3 oz.
170 =	6		$1\frac{1}{2}$ kilo =	3 lb. 5 oz.
175 =	$6\frac{1}{4}$		2 kilos =	4 lb. 6 oz.
185 =	$6\frac{1}{2}$			

Approximate equivalents in volume of the most frequently used ingredients:

Weights and Measures

Sugar	1 lb.	or	450 grams	= 2 cups
	2 oz.	or	60 grams	= $\frac{1}{4}$ cup
Flour	1 lb.	or	450 grams	= 4 cups
(sifted)	2 oz.	or	60 grams	= $\frac{1}{2}$ cup
			100 grams	= $\frac{3}{4}$ cup
Butter	1 lb.	or	450 grams	= 2 cups
	2 oz.	or	60 grams	= $\frac{1}{4}$ cup
			100 grams	= $\frac{1}{3}$ cup less 1 tablespoon

For volume measures, a cup in this book generally means a teacup unless otherwise modified. A full level teacup holds almost the 8 fl. oz. of the standard U.S. measuring cup.

The English tablespoon and the Greek soupspoon are large spoons equal to 4 teaspoons. The U.S. standard measuring tablespoon equals 3 teaspoons.

OVEN COOKING

Traditional Greek oven cooking is done in a beehive-shaped structure usually situated at the side of the house or in the courtyard known as the *avli*.

In the country and the islands those families who have no oven of their own send their food to be cooked in the local bakery and it is a common sight to see the Sunday dinner being carried to the *fourno* in the early morning and home again at noon.

The beehive-shaped oven has a triangular opening which can be closed with a tin sheet propped against it. The oven is stuffed with brushwood which is then set alight and the opening closed with the metal sheet. When the fire has died down it is raked out and the roast, or whatever dish is to be baked, is put in the oven and left there until it is cooked or on baking day it will be put in after the loaves of bread have been taken out.

The roasting-tin used is round and shallow which fits easily into the round interior of the oven and is called a *tapsi*. This is a very useful part of the Greek kitchen equipment and is used for baked dishes of all kinds. The traditional New Year and Easter cakes are always baked in a *tapsi*.

The white wood ash left when the fire has died down is called *stakti* and is used in the country for soaking linen to keep it white. Even in Athens, washerwomen still visit the houses once a month to do the sheets, pillow cases and table linen with *stakti* but with the advent of washing machines, bleaches and detergents this practice is fast dying out.

I

HERBS

He who wishes not to spoil the dishes
Served up to others, should be pleased himself.
For he who rightly cares for his own eating
Will not be a bad cook.

Athenaeus

———————

Although many wild herbs are gathered in the springtime on the stony hillsides of Greece not all have a culinary purpose. The best known and most frequently used is *rigani* (*Origanum Pulchrum*) and any visitor to Greece will long remember this aromatic herb which flavoured the *keftethes* he was served with his *ouzo* in a country *taverna*.

ANITHO   DILL

Dill is used extensively during the rather mild winter enjoyed in Greece and in the spring. Greengrocers sell it in bunches along with spring onions, bunches of parsley and celery tops. Strangely enough, it is always used fresh and the seeds are never dried for kitchen use as in other countries. It is used for various meat, fish and vegetable dishes and will grow even luxuriantly in English gardens. It prefers a dry soil and a sunny corner of the garden.

CAPARI   CAPERS

Capers grow wild in the countryside. They are gathered in

the autumn and pickled in wine vinegar for use during the coming year. They are used to garnish boiled fish, crawfish or octopus dressed with oil and lemon. In the winter they add piquancy to cabbage salads, and in the summer to tomato and cucumber salads.

CHAMOMILE   CHAMOMILE

Chamomile has the same spelling in English but a different pronunciation. It grows very happily everywhere in Greece and in the spring carpets of the flowers are to be seen as commonly as daisies in England. They are gathered and spread out to dry in the hot sun, then stored in airtight jars or, nowadays, cellophane bags, for the winter to make a *tisane* against chills, colds, and stomach upsets. Doctors prescribe Chamomile tea for compresses, eye baths and as a bedtime drink to induce sleep.

The name is sometimes, though incorrectly, spelled 'Camomile'.

DAPHNI   BAY

The bay tree flourishes in Greece in both tree and bush form and grows to quite a height. The leaves are widely used in Greek cooking and it is just as natural for a Greek cook to go into the garden for fresh bay leaves as for an English cook to run out for a few sprigs of mint. Bay leaves are also dried and sold in grocers' shops. Bay leaves have other uses apart from cooking. Before the days of washing machines and indeed even today in country districts, branches of bay are boiled and the water is used as a last rinse for table and bed linen. It imparts a deliciously clean smell to the sheets.

DENDROLIVANO   ROSEMARY

Rosemary grows very profusely in all parts of Greece but is not used very much in Greek cooking, although a sprig or two is sometimes inserted under the skin of lamb before roasting. Water in which a handful of rosemary has been boiled is very useful for freshening up black dresses after washing.

FASKOMILO   SAGE

Sage grows wild on the Greek mountains. I have gathered pungent branches of it on the slopes of Mount Parnassos above Delphi, dried it in the hot sun and preserved it until Christmas Day, when it has given a special flavour to our turkey.

The only use most Greek cooks have for sage is to brew a tea for settling an upset stomach. They are horrified to hear that in England it is used in a stuffing for roast duck, pork, and even the Christmas turkey.

KIMINO   CUMIN

Cumin, although indigenous to Greece, is rarely used in the kitchen. It is, however, well known throughout the country for its medicinal properties and is often used by mothers to infuse along with other seeds into a kind of gripe water for their babies. The only culinary uses I can discover are for flavouring *Soudzoukakia* (Smyrna sausages) and *Stifatho* (Stew).

MAIDANO   PARSLEY

Parsley is one of the most widely used herbs in Greek cooking. I can think of few made dishes which do not require chopped parsley and as it grows all the year round in Greece, there is no need to dry it for use.

MANTZOURANA   MARJORAM

While pot marjoram (*Origanum onites*) and sweet marjoram (*O. majorana*) are to be found growing in Greece, they are, as far as I have been able to ascertain, never used in Greek cooking.

Herbs

RIGANI ORIGANUM PULCHRUM

Origanum comes from two ancient Greek words: *oros*, mountain, and *ganos*, brightness. It grows wild on the mountains of Greece and is probably the most widely used of all herbs in Greek country cooking. A tomato salad, lamb chop or grilled fish will always be served with a sprinkling of *rigani* and while the discreet use of such a pungent herb lends enchantment to the common rissole, a heavy hand with it will murder the subtlety of any dish.

Rigani is widely used in Italy and America under the name of origano. It can be obtained in London. The nearest British substitute would be Winter Savory which grows cheerfully in my own Oxfordshire garden. Marjoram is often mistakenly given in cookery books as a substitute for *rigani*.

SELINO CELERY

Crisp, crunchy sticks of celery are rarely found in Greece. Probably the climate is too mild, but celery leaves are widely used for flavouring. Fish soup would not be complete without the flavour of a bunch of celery tops which are used along with other vegetables to garnish the fish before sending to the table.

While celery is not strictly speaking a herb, it serves the same purpose in the Greek kitchen.

THIOSMOS MINT

Mint is widely used in meat and vegetable dishes. I have only found the well-known spearmint with its sharp pointed, darkly veined leaves growing in Greece. It is frequently used with parsley and *rigani*. Mint tea is a safe cure for indigestion.

THYMARI THYME

Thyme is rarely used in cooking, but after the first rains in September snails are collected on the hillsides, placed in a crock and are left there with branches of thyme to feed upon for several days. This gives them a specially sweet and pleasant flavour before cooking.

Thyme is also put into an earthenware crock together with olives which are being preserved in oil.

TILIO   LIME FLOWERS

In Greece as in France lime tea is a very popular bedtime drink. It calms the nerves and therefore induces sleep. It is also considered to be very good for sore throats and coughs.

VASSILIKOS   BASIL

A pot of sweet basil is nearly always to be found growing on the balcony, terrace or in the courtyards of island and country houses. It is said to keep flies and mosquitoes away and I have often seen it flourishing in the open window of a butcher's shop, presumably for this very purpose. A sprig or two is frequently given in place of a few flowers when visiting country folk, as a gesture of hospitality. In cooking, however, it is confined to flavouring preserves.

II

APPETIZERS AND HORS D'ŒUVRE

*All fish and every meat and herb we eat
Have different qualities at different seasons
Of the revolving year, and he who knows
The principles and reasons of these things
Will use each meat when it is most in season.*

Athenaeus

Enshrined in the ancestral wisdom of the Greeks revealed by trial and perhaps even more clearly by error is the desirability of taking solid food when drinking. The unmistakable authority of the national aperitif, *ouzo*, probably has a great deal to do with this. Except on the fairly numerous festal occasions when to be aggressively sober is in doubtful taste, Greeks are rarely seen affected except for the better by liquor. *Mezethakia* have become a pleasure as well as a precaution.

Even in the simplest wayside *tavernas* you will be served a few olives, a finger or two of cucumber, a pickled pepper or small pieces of bread and cheese with your *ouzo*, but the variety is almost limitless. If the *taverna* is by the sea, you will find delicious fried *marithes* (whitebait) and *kithonia* (clams) sprinkled with lemon juice, or small pieces of boiled octopus and fried *kalamarakia* (baby squid). Any tit-bit that can be served with a drink between meals becomes a *meze*; it can be

34

hot or cold, simple or complicated and puts Greece high in the international *hors-d'œuvre* league.

In Spetsai Crisulla would fry the ink of an octopus in olive oil and with a squeeze of lemon juice serve it with some of her home-baked bread fresh from the oven. Or perhaps she would give us the sweet, orange-coloured roe of the sea urchins we had gathered on the rocks that morning. This is best eaten with a slice of lemon and brown bread. Liver also makes a good appetizer and it is rarely possible to find young calves' liver in a Greek butcher's shop. It will have been snapped up in the market by the *taverna*-keepers for *mezes*.

Taramosalata (Fish Roe Pâté) and *Melitzanosalata* (Aubergine Salad), for which recipes are given, besides making a good first course to a meal are also popular *mezethes*. Indeed almost anything eatable which human ingenuity can serve on toast or a dry biscuit can be a *meze*.

BOUREKAKIA   SMALL SAVOURY PASTIES

Bourekakia is a word of Turkish origin used in Greece as a general term covering all the little savoury-filled pasties of different shapes and sizes such as *kreatopitakia* with a meat filling, *spanakopitakia* when spinach is used, *tiropitakia* made with *fetta* cheese, and *kotopitakia* if the filling is of chicken. They are made with a paper-thin pastry called *filo*, which can be bought at any Greek food shop in London or wherever there is a Greek community. *Filo* can also be made at home and a recipe is given, but it can never be rolled out to the same wafer-like thinness as the bought variety. Flaky pastry, too, can be used but in this case the *bourekakia* are made in the shape of thin sausage rolls or small turnovers.

DOLMATHAKIA   SMALL STUFFED VINE LEAVES

Even in Greece few people today make their own *dolmathakia mezethes*. They are fiddling things to make and can be bought anywhere in tins ready for immediate use. They are eaten cold and go very well with *ouzo*, the aniseed-flavoured national aperitif. If you wish to make them at home, however, follow the recipe for *dolmathes* but make them as tiny as you can.

GARITHES TIGANITES FRIED PRAWNS

Prawns have such a delicate flavour that if they are washed thoroughly as they must be, then boiled in water, they tend to become quite tasteless. When they are very fresh they may be shelled before cooking, but if they have been on ice for a time it is better to put them in a pan without water and let them sweat for ten minutes over a low flame, shaking the pan from time to time to ensure even cooking. When cool enough to handle, remove the shells and use as follows.

Make a light batter with four level tablespoons of flour, one tablespoon of olive oil, a good pinch of salt and about half a cup of warm water. Beat well and stand aside for at least one hour. Just before using fold in the stiffly beaten whites of two eggs. Coat each prawn with batter and drop into a pan of very hot olive oil. Drain and serve immediately.

KEFTETHAKIA SMALL MEAT BALLS

Keftethakia are probably the most popular of all *mezethes* and no Greek cocktail party would be complete without a dish of them. They can be quite delicious if they are well made and served really hot, and equally nasty if care has not been taken in their preparation. Use the recipe for *keftethes* but make them the size of large marbles.

KREATOPITAKIA MEAT PASTIES

For the filling, add one tablespoon of grated onion, two tablespoons of tomato juice and a pinch of cinnamon or a little grated nutmeg to half a pound of finely minced meat and season with salt and pepper. Melt one ounce of unsalted butter in a frying-pan and *sauté* the meat gently for fifteen minutes, adding a little water if too dry. Allow to cool before using, then proceed as with *tiropitakia*.

MELITZANES ME XITHI   AUBERGINE PICKLE

For pickling choose long aubergines and not the round variety.

Make an incision on each side of the aubergines, plunge into boiling water and steep for a few minutes, then pour off the water and drain.

Have ready some coarsely chopped red peppers, celery leaves and stalks, garlic cloves and mint leaves. Mix them all together and stuff the aubergines, tying them up if necessary with strips of celery stalk. Place in an earthenware crock and cover with wine vinegar. They will be ready for use in one week.

MELITZANES SALATA   AUBERGINE SALAD

Besides serving as an appetizer *melitzanes salata* makes a very good first course and is a useful addition to a cold buffet. The round, dark, shiny aubergine is better for this dish, but the long variety may be used if the round kind is not available. I have given two recipes, each prepared differently and with a flavour of its own.

3 lb. aubergines	½ pint olive oil
2 tablespoons grated onion	¼ tablespoon wine vinegar
1 or 2 tablespoons lemon juice	½ teaspoon rigani (*optional*)
1 large ripe tomato	Salt and pepper

Put the aubergines in a moderate oven and leave them until the skins wrinkle and they are soft to touch. When cool enough to handle peel them and remove as many seeds as possible. Pound the onion to pulp with a pinch of salt and beat in the flesh of the aubergines with some of the lemon juice, working quickly as the flesh of an aubergine discolours and darkens easily on exposure to the air. Next put in the skinned and chopped tomato and continue to beat until well blended and smooth. Add the *rigani*, more salt if necessary and a grind or two of pepper and work in the olive oil and more lemon juice until the mixture is thick and creamy. At the last moment mix in the wine vinegar, garnish with thinly sliced green peppers and chill well before serving.

MELITZANES SALATA (2)   AUBERGINE SALAD

This is Crisulla's recipe for *melitzanes salata* and a less refined version of the preceding recipe, though equally good and perhaps even better for those who like garlic. I give it just as she gave it to me.

3 *lb. aubergines*	½ *pint olive oil*
1 *large onion*	1 *tablespoon chopped parsley*
3 *cloves garlic*	1 *teaspoon chopped mint*
½ *cup breadcrumbs*	½ *teaspoon* rigani
1 *tablespoon lemon juice*	½ *teaspoon dry mustard*
3 *tablespoons wine vinegar*	*Salt and pepper*

Choose round, plump plants and put them in a moderate oven until the skins wrinkle and they seem soft to the touch. Allow them to cool a little, then pass through a fine mincer, together with the onion, garlic, breadcrumbs, mint, parsley and *rigani*. Season to taste with salt, pepper and mustard. Work in the olive oil and vinegar as if making mayonnaise and add the lemon juice last. Chill and serve garnished with sliced tomatoes and green peppers.

OCTAPOTHI VRASTO   BOILED OCTOPUS

When a live octopus comes from the sea, it is brown and yellow in colour and most unappetizing to look at. Savage as it may seem the octopus has to be beaten and rubbed on a rock or rough-surfaced stone to make it tender and fit to eat.

In the Greek islands it is a common sight to see a fisherman flinging his freshly caught octopus sharply on the ground as many as twenty times before he begins to rub it with a circular movement on the rough surface of the rock until it exudes a frothy lather and gradually changes colour to pearly grey and becomes almost translucent. Experience tells him when he has beaten and rubbed enough to make it ready for the pot. An octopus sold at a fishmongers is always ready for cooking and may be tested for tenderness by tearing at one of the tentacles near the body. When cooked it has something of the texture of lobster and a delicate flavour of its own.

Wash a well-flayed octopus, changing the water several times before removing the ink. Put it into a pan of boiling salted water and simmer gently about one hour or until tender. Remove from the pan to drain and cool, when it should be cut into pieces from one to two inches long and put into a shallow bowl. Pour over some olive oil and lemon juice or wine vinegar and strew with *rigani*.

The ink of the octopus, fried in very hot olive oil, with a squeeze of lemon juice and seasoned with salt and pepper makes a delicious *meze* served with wholemeal bread.

SAGANAKI   FRIED CHEESE

In Greek *tavernas* a popular savoury is prepared by cutting fairly thick slices of hard cheese, *kefalotiri* or *kasseri* being most frequently used. Dust the slices of cheese with flour and fry in small individual two-handled frying-pans in which a little fresh butter has been heated. Add a squeeze of lemon juice and serve piping hot.

SIKOTAKIA TIGANITA   FRIED LIVER

Cut some lambs' or calves' liver into small pieces and fry them quickly in butter. Add a squeeze of lemon juice and serve piping hot on cocktail sticks.

SPANAKOPITAKIA SPINACH PASTIES

To prepare the filling for *spanakopitakia* chop two pounds of spinach, using the leaves only, with six spring onions and cook together until soft. Mash four ounces of *fetta* cheese, add one dessertspoon of chopped dill or fennel and bind together with half a pint of Béchamel sauce, although this is optional. Use the same amount of *filo* or pastry and proceed as for *tiropitakia*.

TARAMOSALATA FISH ROE PÂTÉ

Taramosalata is a creamy fish roe *pâté* and the basic ingredient is *tarama*, the salted and pressed roe of the grey mullet or cod which comes from Scandinavia and Russia and is imported in bulk in barrels. It is obtainable at any Greek delicatessen shop. I have given two recipes. The first quickly made and served more usually in the country or in the islands and the second a more refined version which takes longer to prepare but which makes a very good luncheon first course as well as *meze* served on small squares of bread or toast.

Dip two ounces of *tarama* in water and leave for a few minutes to remove some of the salt. Squeeze out any excessive moisture and using a pestle and mortar or a bowl and a wooden spoon, work to a fine creamy consistency adding one breakfast cup of olive oil and the juice of one or two lemons slowly and steadily as if making mayonnaise. Mix in two or three finely sliced spring onions and one teaspoon of chopped dill and serve with fresh crusty brown bread.

There are so many ways of making *taramosalata* that it is quite worth experimenting with the various ingredients until you find a variation that suits you. Some people like a lot of onion, some like a little and others none at all. Some Greek cooks use only potato and no bread, others all bread and no potato and yet others use both. This recipe is one I use regularly and like best after trying all the variations.

4 oz. tarama
1 *tablespoon grated onion*
1 *boiled floury potato*

1 *slice stale bread 2 to 3 in.*
  thick
Juice of 1 or 2 lemons
¾ *pint olive oil*

Soak the *tarama* in water to remove some of the salt, cut the crusts from the bread, dip the rest in water and squeeze dry. Pound the grated onion to a pulp then put in the *tarama* and pound well together. Next add the boiled potato and work that well in, then the bread and continue to work until the ingredients are well mixed and a smooth consistency is reached. Now add the oil and lemon juice alternately, little by little as if making mayonnaise, until the colour is a very pale pink and the texture is light and fluffy. Garnish with black olives before serving.

TIRAKIA   FRIED CHEESE

Apart from the famous *fetta*, a somewhat soft and crumbly white cheese made from sheep's milk, there are several hard goats'-milk cheeses. Among these, *kefalotiri* and *kasseri* are good cooking cheeses used mainly for grating and serving with macaroni or a *pilafe*, although the more well-to-do Athenian nowadays buys Parmesan because of its fuller flavour. When buying Greek cheeses it is as well to taste them all as the salt content varies considerably. There is not much to choose between any of them but cut into small squares and either fried in hot olive oil or put under the grill for a minute until browned slightly, then served on cocktail sticks with a squeeze of lemon juice, they make pleasant *mezes*.

TIRAKIA TIGANITA   CHEESE PUFFS

Beat two egg whites until they form peaks and fold in as much finely grated *kefalotiri* or Parmesan cheese and a grind of pepper as the egg whites will take to form small balls. As they are made, drop them into a deep pan of very hot olive oil and fry quickly. Serve before they go leathery.

TIROPITAKIA   CHEESE PASTIES

Mash half a pound of *fetta* cheese with a fork and mix with two well-beaten eggs, one dessertspoon of finely chopped parsley and a grind of freshly milled pepper.

Cut eight sheets of *filo* into long strips about two and a half inches wide and brush each strip with olive oil or melted butter. Put one teaspoon of the filling on one end of a strip and fold over, continuing to fold from side to side to the other end, making a small triangular packet. When all the *filo* and the filling has been used in this way, put the *tiropitakia* on a well-greased baking-sheet, brush them over lightly again with olive oil or melted butter and bake in a moderate oven until crisp and golden. They are also good fried in a deep pan of very hot olive oil, but should be drained well before serving piping hot.

III

SAUCES AND DRESSINGS

Know that in the cookery no seasoning
Is equal to the sauce of impudence.

Athenaeus

———

Sauces are much used in Greek cooking but the variety is limited. Oil, onions, tomatoes, eggs, lemons and garlic all play a big part combined with native herbs such as parsley, bay and the pungent *rigani* to make spicy sauces to serve with meat, fish and vegetable dishes.

The three main cooked sauces are tomato sauce, egg and lemon sauce, and a basic Béchamel sauce, to which are added eggs and cheese, according to the requirements of the dish.

For fresh salads, cooked vegetable salads and fish, *lathoxitho* (sauce vinaigrette) and *latholemono* (oil and lemon sauce), mayonnaise or a garlic sauce known as *skorthalia* are used most frequently.

Mayonnaise and Béchamel are of course not Greek but of French origin. Mayonnaise was invented in 1756 by the chef of the Duc de Richelieu who was at the time in command of the French Army besieging Port Mahon in Minorca; hence the original name 'Mahonnaise'.

Béchamel sauce was named and created by Louis de Béchamel, Marquis de Nointel, Lord Steward and Maître d'Hôtel of the Household at the Court of Louis XIV.

AVGOLEMONO SALTSA   <small>EGG AND LEMON SAUCE</small>

This is a basic recipe for the famous *avgolemono* sauce used with so many meat and vegetable dishes in Greece.

1 *oz. butter*	2 *eggs*
2 *level tablespoons flour*	*Juice of* 1 *or* 2 *lemons as liked*
½ *pint hot stock*	2 *tablespoons cold water*

Make a *roux* with the butter and flour and cook for a few minutes before adding the hot stock very slowly, stirring all the time to prevent the sauce from becoming lumpy. Keep hot while preparing the eggs and the lemon. Beat the eggs until light and frothy and, while still beating, add the lemon juice and then the cold water. Now add the hot stock, a ladleful at a time and return to the pan, taking care that once the hot stock has been added to the egg and lemon it is not allowed to boil or the sauce will curdle.

BÉCHAMEL SALTSA   <small>WHITE SAUCE</small>

This is a basic white sauce used extensively, with the addition of eggs and cheese, in the preparation of many national dishes.

2 *oz. butter*	1½ *pints milk*
2 *level tablespoons flour*	*Salt, pepper and nutmeg*

Melt the butter in a heavy-bottomed pan and add the flour gradually, stirring continuously to prevent burning. Stir in the warmed milk very slowly, keeping the sauce smooth until the desired consistency is reached. Add salt, pepper and grated nutmeg according to the requirements of the dish with which the sauce is to be used.

DOMATA SALTSA   <small>TOMATO SAUCE</small>

A plain easily made tomato sauce to serve with a *pilafe,*

macaroni and many other dishes. If fresh tomatoes are not available, tinned tomatoes or tomato paste diluted with a little water may be used instead.

2 *lb. ripe tomatoes*	1 *bay leaf*
2 *oz. butter*	1 *sprig sweet basil*
2 *heaped tablespoons grated onion*	1 *wineglass red wine*
	½ *pint water*
1 *level dessertspoon sugar*	*Salt and pepper*
½ *teaspoon powdered cinnamon* (*or* 1 *stick*)	

Skin the tomatoes and put them through a coarse sieve to reduce them to a *purée* and remove the seeds. Melt the butter in a heavy pan, add the onion, tomatoes, herbs and seasoning and cook for fifteen minutes before adding the water and the wine. Simmer gently over a low flame for another thirty minutes when the sauce should have thickened slightly and be ready to use. Remove the bay leaf, sweet basil and stick of cinnamon before serving.

DOMATA SALTSA ME KIMA
TOMATO SAUCE WITH MINCED VEAL

The same ingredients are used as for the preceding recipe with the addition of one pound of finely minced veal. The onion should be softened in butter and a little water before the meat is added and cooked slowly for at least fifteen minutes before putting in the tomatoes, herbs and seasoning. Add the wine and simmer for about one hour.

SALTSA ME SICOTI   TOMATO SAUCE WITH LIVER

Instead of minced veal use the same amount of calves' liver cut into small pieces. Fry the onion lightly in butter and brown the liver to seal the juices before adding the tomatoes, herbs, seasoning, wine and water. If a richer sauce is liked, add a small glass of vermouth or cooking brandy just before removing from the fire.

Both the above sauces served with a *pilafe* or spaghetti make a good luncheon main course.

LATHOLEMONO   OLIVE OIL AND LEMON SAUCE

This sauce is served with boiled or grilled fish and often with lobster as an alternative to mayonnaise. The unsuspecting traveller in Greece ordering a grilled fish in a *taverna* is frequently horrified to find it served on a plate swimming in oil and lemon juice. It is very good if you like olive oil, but it is better to help oneself from a sauceboat.

   ½ pint olive oil   *1 tablespoon chopped parsley*
   2 tablespoons lemon juice   *Salt and pepper to taste*

Beat the olive oil with the lemon juice until thoroughly combined. Add the parsley, salt and pepper and serve immediately as the olive oil and lemon juice will separate if allowed to stand.

LATHI KAI LEMONI
OLIVE OIL AND LEMON DRESSING

This dressing is widely used for both winter and summer salads and any green vegetable which can be boiled and left to go cold constitutes a salad.

Mix three tablespoons of olive oil with one tablespoon of lemon juice and add salt and pepper. Pour over any salad, either cooked or raw.

LATHI KAI XITHI
OLIVE OIL AND VINEGAR DRESSING

Used as an alternative dressing for uncooked salads only but never with a raw cabbage salad, when oil and lemon is used for this most popular of all winter salads.

Mix one tablespoon of olive oil with one teaspoon of wine vinegar and add salt and pepper to taste. Beat well and when thoroughly combined, pour over the salad. When used for a lettuce salad, mix the dressing in the bowl in which the salad is to be served. Toss in the lettuce, turning the leaves gently with a wooden spoon so that the lettuce becomes coated with the dressing and none remains in the bowl.

MAYONAISA MAYONNAISE

Most people have their own particular recipe for making mayonnaise and the Greeks are no exception. The main difference is that lemon juice is used instead of vinegar and a jelly-like consistency is achieved by the proportionate amounts of olive oil and lemon juice used to each egg yolk.

Yolk of 1 egg
1½ cups olive oil
1 or 2 tablespoons lemon juice

½ teaspoon sugar
½ teaspoon dry mustard (if liked)
Salt and pepper

Use a smooth bowl or basin and a wooden spoon and remember that a good mayonnaise is achieved by slow, steady stirring. Put the salt, pepper, sugar and mustard, if used, in the bowl and break in the yolk of egg. Stir strongly and evenly for a few minutes, then start adding the oil drop by drop until half a cupful has been absorbed. Add the lemon juice and the rest of the oil alternately until the desired consistency and flavour is reached. Should the mayonnaise curdle, start again with a clean bowl and another egg yolk and gradually work in the curdled mayonnaise.

SKORTHALIA GARLIC SAUCE

This is Crisulla's island recipe for *skorthalia* and for those who really like garlic it is excellent with fried fish, fried aubergine slices or baby marrows sliced and fried in olive oil. It can be made with either boiled potatoes or bread. If bread is used the crusts should be removed and the bread soaked in water for two minutes, then squeezed dry in the hand. If you are making it with potatoes, boil them in their jackets and peel them before use.

6 *or* 8 *cloves of garlic*	1 *pint olive oil*
5 *medium size potatoes or*	1 *tablespoon wine vinegar or*
2 *slices stale bread about*	*lemon juice*
2 *in. thick*	*Salt as required*

Put the cleaned garlic cloves through a fine mincer with the bread or potatoes, then remove to a mortar and pound well until quite smooth. Add the olive oil and lemon juice or vinegar slowly as if for mayonnaise and when absorbed, stir in a small coffee cup of cold water. Serve with a beetroot salad.

Someone once told me that a clove of garlic swallowed whole before eating a garlic dish will prevent the lingering and objectionable smell on the breath. I tried this out one day at an island luncheon party before my guests left for Athens. We all ate *skorthalia* and one of the guests experimented by swallowing a clove whole before he began his lunch. True enough, on arrival in Athens that evening he was the only one of the party whose breath was not offensive to those who had not eaten garlic that day.

IV

MACARONI AND RICE DISHES

Tho' the cook was good, 'twas
Attic salt that flavoured best the food.

To Atticus from Cicero.   45 B.C.

MACARONIA ME DOMATA SALTSA
SPAGHETTI WITH TOMATO SAUCE

2½ lb. spaghetti
4 oz. butter

6 oz. grated cheese (kefalotiri, kasseri or Parmesan)
Tomato Sauce (see 'Sauces')

Cook the spaghetti in plenty of boiling salted water. Drain well and return to the pan. Melt the butter separately and when bubbling, but before it colours, pour it on to the spaghetti. Toss over a low flame for a few minutes and pile on to a serving dish. Sprinkle with grated cheese and pour a little of the sauce on the top to garnish. Serve the sauce separately with a bowl of grated cheese.

MACARONIA ME KIMA
SPAGHETTI WITH MINCED MEAT SAUCE

2½ lb. spaghetti
1 lb. minced veal
3 onions
½ pint olive oil
1½ lb. ripe tomatoes or 1
   large tin tomatoes
1 tablespoon tomato paste
3 cloves garlic

1 bay leaf
Cinnamon
Sugar
Salt and pepper
1 wineglass white wine
6 oz. grated cheese, Parmesan or kefalotiri

D

49

To make the sauce, chop the onions finely and cook them gently in a little water and olive oil. Add the minced meat and stir with a wooden spoon to prevent burning. Add the sieved tomatoes, tomato paste, sliced garlic, bay leaf, cinnamon and sugar. Season with salt and pepper and stew gently for one hour when the sauce should be thick. Ten minutes before serving add the wine.

Boil the spaghetti in boiling salted water and drain. Return to the pan and toss it in butter. Pile on a serving dish and sprinkle with grated cheese. Serve the sauce separately with a dish of grated cheese.

PASTICCIO   BAKED MACARONI WITH MINCED MEAT

2 *lb. macaroni*
1½ *lb. minced meat*
1 *onion*
1 *teaspoon sugar*
4 *ripe tomatoes,* 1 *small tin tomatoes or* 1 *good tablespoon tomato paste*
4 *oz. Butter*

1 *pint Béchamel sauce (see* 'Sauces')
4 *eggs*
8 *oz. grated cheese* (kefalotiri *or Parmesan*)
½ *teaspoon cinnamon*
Nutmeg
Salt and pepper

Put the minced meat into a pan with the finely chopped onion, a grate of nutmeg, a pinch of cinnamon, salt, pepper and sugar and a generous knob of butter. Stir well and cook over a low flame for twenty minutes. When slightly browned, add the sieved tomatoes and two tablespoons of water and cook gently for a further twenty minutes. Remove from the flame and mix in two good tablespoons of Béchamel sauce.

Cook the macaroni in plenty of boiling salted water until soft but firm. Drain well and return to the pan. Heat the rest of the butter and pour over the macaroni.

Have ready a well-buttered fireproof dish and line the bottom with half the macaroni. Sprinkle with cheese then spread the meat and the rest of the macaroni. Add more cheese and cover with the Béchamel sauce into which you have beaten the four eggs. Put the remainder of the cheese on top and cook in a moderately hot oven until brown and crusty.

TIROPITTA   CHEESE PIE

 1 *lb.* fetta *cheese*   *Pepper and nutmeg*
 3 *or* 4 *eggs*   *Olive oil*
 1½ *pints Béchamel sauce (see* 12 *oz.* filo (*pastry sheets*)
 'Sauces')

Mash the *fetta* cheese with a fork and combine with the well-beaten eggs and Béchamel sauce. Season to taste. Smooth half the pastry sheets into an oiled baking-tin, brushing each sheet with olive oil as they are smoothed one on another. Pour in the filling and cover with the remaining oiled pastry sheets. Score the top into squares with a sharp knife or razor blade, cover with greaseproof paper and bake in a moderate oven until golden and crisp. About one hour.

Cut into squares before serving.

PILAFE

This is a basic recipe for cooking rice and is served with different trimmings and sauces, variations of which may occur to the cook.

Melt one ounce of butter in a saucepan over a brisk fire and add five cups of hot water and salt to taste. When the water has reached boiling point throw in two cups of cleaned rice and stir well once only or the rice will clog. Keep on a brisk fire until the rice swells and the water evaporates. When most of the water has been driven off or absorbed by the rice, cover the saucepan with a clean cloth, put on the pan lid and leave on a very low fire for half an hour.

When ready to serve, melt another two ounces of butter and while still bubbling, pour over the rice. Press the rice into a mould and turn out to serve.

PILAFE ME DOMATES GLACE

TOMATOES WITH RICE

In Greek homes, a frequently served first course is glazed tomatoes and rice. The tomatoes should be of the small, long variety and should be peeled before cooking. They are also obtainable ready peeled in tins.

Put the tomatoes into a frying-pan with a little water and bring to the boil. Add a good knob of butter and one tablespoon of sugar to one pound of tomatoes. Cook very slowly until the sauce is thick and glazed. Have ready a plain *pilafe* and form into individual moulds by packing the cooked rice into a cup. Turn out on to a serving dish and top the rice with the glazed tomatoes.

PILAFE ME DOMATA SALTSA

RICE WITH TOMATO SAUCE

Make a *pilafe*, allowing half a teacup of rice to one and a half of water for each person. Individual portions can be served by pressing the cooked rice into a breakfast cup before turning out on to individual plates.

Make a rich tomato sauce for which a recipe is given. Pour a tablespoonful over each mould and serve the rest in a sauce boat. Serve with a bowl of grated Parmesan cheese.

If liked, small pieces of lambs' or calves' liver may be cooked in the sauce.

PILAFE ME GARITHES

PRAWNS WITH RICE

3 *pints prawns*
1 *small onion*
2 *cloves garlic (if liked)*
2 *oz. butter*
1 *cup tomato pulp*
1 *sprig rosemary or sweet basil*
1 *teaspoon sugar*
½ *wineglass vermouth*
½ *wineglass cream*
A pinch of cinnamon
Salt and pepper

Prepare the prawns as for *garithes vrastes* (see page 70). Scrape out the heads and keep on one side. Chop the onion and garlic very finely and *sauté* gently in butter until quite soft, then add the scrapings from the prawns' heads, the tomato pulp, sugar, cinnamon, rosemary or sweet basil and season with salt and pepper. Simmer slowly for half an hour, remove from the fire and pass through a fine sieve. Return to the pan and put in the prawns with the vermouth and cream and reheat. Have ready a *pilafe*. Press the rice into a ring mould before turning out on to the serving dish. Fill the centre with the prawns and serve hot.

PILAFE ME JAMBON KAI ARAKA
RICE WITH HAM AND GREEN PEAS

A popular variation is to cut some lean boiled ham into very small pieces and *sauté* them in butter with some cooked garden peas. When thoroughly warmed, fork into the *pilafe* before forming into a mould.

PILAFE ME OCTAPOTHI   OCTOPUS WITH RICE

1 *small octopus*   1 *dessertspoon tomato paste*
1 *finely chopped onion*   6 *oz. rice*
¼ *pint olive oil*   *Salt and pepper*
2 *large ripe tomatoes or*

Wash the octopus well, remove the ink sac and keep on one side. Cut the octopus into small pieces and put into a pan without water and leave over a small flame to draw the liquid from the octopus. When the liquid has been re-absorbed add the onion and olive oil and cook gently for ten or fifteen minutes. Next add the chopped and skinned tomatoes or the tomato paste diluted with water and the ink from the octopus. Add enough water to cover and cook until the octopus is quite tender. Throw in the rice and cook rapidly until all the liquid in the pan has been absorbed. Place a dry clean cloth over the pan and leave aside from the fire to draw the steam for ten minutes before serving.

PILAFE ME ORTIKIA QUAIL WITH RICE

6 *or* 8 *quail*	1 *wineglass of red or white*
1 *tablespoon olive oil*	*wine*
2 *oz. butter*	*Boiled rice*
¼ *pint water*	*Salt and pepper*

Put the birds into a shallow earthenware dish with the olive oil, butter, wine and water, season to taste and cover with a close-fitting lid. Cook slowly in a moderate oven until tender. When ready to serve, arrange them on a bed of rice and pour over the juices left in the baking-dish.

PILAFE ME SIKOTI RICE WITH LIVER

Prepare a *pilafe*. Cut some lambs' or calves' liver into small pieces the size of a walnut, allowing four ounces for each person. Fry them in butter and put them on top of the moulded rice. Serve with a bowl of yoghourt.

TAS KEBAB MEAT WITH RICE

2 *lb. veal or stewing steak*	1 *wineglass vermouth*
2 *oz. butter*	1 *pint hot water*
2 *finely sliced onions*	1 *teaspoon sugar*
4 *very ripe tomatoes*	*Pinch of cinnamon*
1 *good teaspoon tomato paste*	*Salt and pepper*

Melt the onions in the butter, using a heavy saucepan. Add the skinned and pulped tomatoes, cinnamon, sugar, salt and pepper and the tomato paste diluted in water. Cut the meat into small pieces and put into the pan. Stir in the water, cover the pan and cook very slowly for one hour or until the meat is tender. Just before serving stir in a wineglass of vermouth. Serve with a *pilafe*.

If liked, the rice may be cooked with the meat. In this case more water must be added before throwing in the rice.

V

SOUPS

We may live without poetry, music and art;
We may live without conscience and live without heart;
We may live without friends; we may live without books,
But civilized man cannot live without cooks.

Athenaeus

One of the directions in which Greek culture influenced Mediterranean thought was in the making of soup. Whatever yells of Chauvinistic rage may arise from Marseilles on account of this statement, there is little doubt that *bouillabaisse* was introduced into France by colonizing Greeks under the name of *kakavia*. Since classical times or perhaps earlier, *kakavia* has been a standby of the island fishermen who may remain at sea for days at a time.

Soup very often constitutes a main dish, some are so substantial and thick that they are a meal in themselves—particularly the bean soups. These winter dishes are eaten largely during Lent when the Greek Orthodox Church frowns on the eating of meat. In ancient times *fassolatha* was a staple winter dish, and it is still a great comfort when the searching north wind comes whistling down over the Attic plain.

The old Athenians had to import a great deal of their food as the soil of Attica was so unproductive. Wheat came from Sicily, peaches from Persia, apricots from Armenia and oranges, it is said, from China, though at some time this business seems to have gone to the Portuguese as oranges are now called *portocalia*.

Soups

Fish soups are very popular. No fish stock is ever thrown away in a Greek kitchen; it makes a wonderful *avgolemono soupa*.

AVGOLEMONO SOUPA EGG AND LEMON SOUP

Avgolemono soup is probably the most popular soup in Greece. It is very simply and quickly made from any white stock and is light, nourishing and easily digested. Fish, chicken or veal stock or even a few bones will provide the basis for a delicious soup fit for the fanciest of dinner parties.

Variations on the basic method of preparing an *avgolemono* soup can be made by substituting a little flour, vermicelli, tapioca or any of the soup *pastas* for the rice.

3 pints stock
A handful of rice
3 eggs
Juice of 1 or 2 lemons
Salt and pepper

Bring the stock to the boil. Throw in a handful of rice, vermicelli, tapioca or any one of the many prepared soup macaronis. Beat the eggs well until frothy and add the lemon juice and a tablespoon of cold water. Next take a ladleful of the hot stock and add it slowly to the egg and lemon. Add another ladleful or two, then pour it all back into the pan and stir well, keeping the soup away from the fire. Serve at once.

Care must be taken not to let the soup boil once the eggs and lemon juice have been added or it will curdle.

If a creamy soup is desired then leave out the rice, etc., and thicken the stock with a little flour or cornflour mixed to a paste with cold water and add it to the stock before combining with the egg and lemon juice.

DOMATOSOUPA TOMATO SOUP

A very delicious and seemingly rich summer soup which can be made without meat stock and when tomatoes are ripe and plentiful.

2 *lb. ripe and juicy tomatoes*
1 *potato*
1 *onion*
1 *baby marrow (if available)*
3 *celery tops*
Water

2 *tablespoons olive oil or*
  butter
1 *teaspoon sugar*
1 *tablespoon sago*
Salt and pepper
Chopped parsley to garnish

Prepare and chop the vegetables rather coarsely and put them all into a pan with about six breakfast cups of water and bring to the boil. Add the olive oil or butter, sugar and seasoning and simmer until soft. Pass through a fine sieve and return to the pan. Bring to the boil once again and when bubbling throw in a tablespoon of *pasta* or fine sago. Simmer for ten minutes and serve garnished with plenty of chopped parsley.

FAKKI   BROWN LENTIL SOUP

1½ *lb. brown lentils*
2 *large onions*
3 *cloves garlic*
4 *tablespoons olive oil*
3 *bay leaves*

1 *dessertspoon flour*
2 *dessertspoons wine vinegar*
4 *pints water*
Salt and pepper

Wash the lentils well and put them into a pan of cold water and bring to the boil. Drain off the water and throw it away. Slice the onions and garlic cloves thinly and add to the contents of the pan with the bay leaves, olive oil and water. Bring to boiling point and simmer gently for about one hour or until the lentils are soft. This depends on the freshness of the lentils. Mix the flour and vinegar to a smooth paste and add to the soup, season to taste and cook for ten more minutes. If liked, two tablespoons of tomato paste may be mixed with the flour and vinegar before adding to the soup.

FASSOLATHA   HARICOT BEAN SOUP

1½ *lb. haricot beans*
1 *large onion*

½ *pint olive oil*
4 *ripe tomatoes (optional)*

57

3 *carrots*
3 *tablespoons chopped celery*
   leaves

4 *pints water*
Salt and pepper

Soak the beans overnight, rinse them well and put them into a pan with enough water to cover. Bring to the boil quickly and simmer for about five minutes, then drain and throw away the water.

Add the finely sliced onion, carrots, celery leaves, olive oil and cover with hot water. Season to taste and cook slowly for about an hour and a half, adding more water from time to time if necessary. If tomatoes are used they should be skinned and pulped before adding to the soup with the seasoning about three-quarters of an hour before serving. If tomatoes are not used cut a lemon into quarters and serve with the soup.

FAVA   YELLOW LENTIL SOUP

1½ *lb. yellow lentils*
1 *large onion*

½ *pint olive oil*
Salt

Wash and cover the lentils with water and bring to the boil. Remove any scum which rises to the surface and when the water is quite clear add the finely chopped onion and olive oil. Simmer slowly for about an hour and a half, adding salt to taste when the lentils have become soft. If the salt is added too soon the lentils will remain hard and be difficult to put through a sieve. This soup should be served in the form of a thick *purée* with a dish of finely chopped raw onion and a cruet of olive oil and lemon juice.

FITHÉ SOUPA   VERMICELLI SOUP

4 *oz. vermicelli*
3 *pints water*

2 *oz. butter*
Lemon juice
Salt

Put the vermicelli into the pan of boiling salted water, add the butter and cook rapidly until soft. Add a squeeze of lemon juice and serve.

This soup should be rather thick and glutinous and is widely used for invalids and children. It is both light and nourishing besides being very quickly made. If a richer soup is desired, veal or chicken stock may be used instead of water. In this case, leave out the butter.

HORTOSOUPA HIMONIATIKI
WINTER VEGETABLE SOUP

2 or 3 onions	3 quarts water
4 cloves garlic	3 tablespoons olive oil or
2 small potatoes	2 oz. butter
2 or 3 carrots	1 tablespoon chopped celery
1 leek	leaves, a little chopped mint,
¼ Savoy cabbage	dill and parsley
Any other green vegetable to hand	2 bay leaves
	Salt and pepper
1 tin tomatoes or 1 tablespoon tomato paste	

Chop the onion and garlic and melt gently in the oil or butter until soft but not coloured. Cut up all the vegetables and add to the onion, putting in first those which take longest to cook such as potatoes and carrots. Turn well in the pan and when beginning to soften add the green vegetables and tomatoes. Cover with water, add seasoning and herbs and simmer gently for about one and a half hours. When the vegetables are all cooked, pass through a coarse sieve and return to the pan for ten minutes before serving.

HORTOSOUPA KALOKAIRIANI
SUMMER VEGETABLE SOUP

1 small onion	2 oz. butter
1 small bunch spring onions	A few fresh beans or peas
1 lettuce	A little chopped mint, parsley,

2 *baby marrows*
¼ *cucumber*
2 *or* 3 *ripe tomatoes if liked*

dill, celery leaves and sweet basil
3 *to* 4 *pints water*
Salt and pepper

Soften the finely sliced onion in butter. Chop and add all the other vegetables, putting in the herbs last. Add a teaspoon of sugar if fresh tomatoes are used as they are inclined to be acid. Cover with at least three pints of water, add salt and pepper, and simmer gently until all the vegetables are soft.

KAKAVIA   GREEK BOUILLABAISSE

I have given the recipe used today in the houses on the islands, but very often the fishermen who go off, sometimes for a month at a time, run out of the small supplies of potatoes, onions and oil they carry with them. Then they make themselves a soup of the various small fish caught in the nets, with plenty of water, lemon juice and nothing else.

Crisulla told me that when she was a child her family used to stay at an isolated beach on the other side of the island for two or three days at a time. Her father loved fishing and spent his days out in a little boat in the bay, coming back sometimes with six or seven pounds of fish of all kinds and sizes. They would then build a fire with driftwood and pine cones, put the catch into a large cooking pot, cover it with water and boil it till the flesh fell away from the bones. Plenty of lemon juice would then be squeezed in and the fish soup, together with a hunk of bread, would be the family supper.

2 *or* 3 *lb. of small varied fish*
2 *onions (or more if very small)*
1 *lb. ripe tomatoes*
2 *potatoes*

Celery tops
½ *pint olive oil*
Salt and pepper
Juice of 2 *lemons*

Put a large pan of water on to boil, together with the oil, onions, potatoes and tomatoes all cut up rather roughly. Add the celery, salt and pepper. Put in the fish and boil without a lid for fifteen to twenty minutes. Before serving squeeze in the juice of two lemons.

Saffron, which is used in the making of a good *bouillabaisse*, was used by the Ancient Greeks in their cooking but it is rarely used in Greece today, although it is well known in Macedonia and Asia Minor.

KOTOSOUPA   CHICKEN SOUP

1 *boiling fowl*	*Rice*
4 *shallots or* 1 *small onion*	*Salt and pepper*
1 *celery top if available*	3 *eggs*
3 *pints water*	*Juice of* 2 *lemons*

Clean, wash and truss the bird, putting one of the shallots or half an onion inside. Put the bird with the other half of the onion or the shallots, celery and seasoning into a large pan and cover with water. Bring to the boil and simmer gently for about two hours according to the size of the bird. When it is cooked, lift out the bird and strain the broth. Return to the pan and reheat. When it is bubbling, throw in a handful of rice and cook for fifteen minutes. Beat the eggs with two tablespoons of cold water and lemon juice until frothy. Now take a ladleful of the hot stock and, stirring constantly, pour it slowly into the egg and lemon. Add another ladleful, then pour it all back into the pan, stirring slowly and taking care not to let the soup boil or it will curdle.

If a cream soup is preferred leave out the rice and mix a tablespoon or two of flour with a little water, adding it to the broth and simmer for a few minutes before pouring into the egg and lemon.

MAYERITSA   EASTER SOUP

For the Greeks, Easter is the most important feast of the year. In northern Europe preparations for Christmas take priority and mincemeat, puddings and the Christmas cake take up a good deal of the housewife's time before the Great Day.

In Greece preparations start about ten days before Easter and towards the end of Holy Week are in full swing. In the Cyclades, houses and even the streets receive their annual coat of whitewash so that they will sparkle in the bright sunlight for Easter Day. In Athens, men armed with five-foot long brushes and pails of whitewash make a round of the houses offering their services in the annual spring clean, although with the increase of flat-dwellers this familiar sight is becoming rarer and rarer.

It is forbidden by law to kill a lamb for a fortnight before Holy Week and most Greeks take their fasting during this last week very seriously. Even *lathero fayeto*, food prepared with olive oil, is taboo and *tarama*, olives, halva and boiled vegetables, together with plenty of onions, garlic and bread sustain the Greek people until midnight on Holy Saturday when the Week's fast is broken without loss of time. Promptly on returning from church at midnight, *mayeritsa*, the traditional Easter soup made from the entrails of the Pascal Lamb, is served to all members of the household.

The heart, liver, lungs and intestine of a young lamb	*A few sprigs mint*
	3 oz. rice
4 pints water	*Salt and pepper*
3 oz. butter	*3 eggs*
12 spring onions	*Juice of 2 lemons*
A small bunch dill or fennel	

To clean the intestine, wash and carefully turn it inside out, using a small thin stick for the purpose. Rub it between the hands with coarse salt and rinse thoroughly. Wash the heart, liver and lungs and put them together with the intestine into a large pan. Cover with water and at boiling point, add salt and simmer gently for about half an hour. Cut up the spring onions, fresh dill and mint very finely. Remove the meat from the pan and keep the stock on one side. Drain the meat and cut it into very small pieces. Melt the butter in a frying-pan and *sauté* the meat, chopped onions and herbs for a few minutes, stirring all the time. Put them back into the pan with the stock, season and simmer for about an hour. When the meat is tender throw in the rice and boil rapidly for fifteen minutes.

Beat the eggs and lemon juice with a little cold water. Add two ladlefuls of the hot broth, one at a time, then pour it all back into the pan and stir well. Reheat if necessary but on no account allow it to boil or the soup will curdle.

PSAROSOUPA   FISH SOUP

Fish soup is nearly always made with egg and lemon juice (see *avgolemono* soup) but this recipe is much used in the islands during the summer when eggs are both dear and scarce.

3 *pints fish stock*	1 *lemon*
1½ *lb. ripe peeled tomatoes or*	2 *tablespoons olive oil*
1 *tablespoon tomato paste*	*Salt and pepper*
3 *oz. rice or tapioca*	*Chopped parsley*

Add the chopped tomatoes or tomato paste and olive oil to the fish stock, season with salt and pepper and simmer for half an hour. Throw in the tapioca or rice and boil rapidly until soft. When the soup is ready, serve with a squeeze of lemon juice and garnish with chopped parsley.

PATSAS   TRIPE SOUP

3 *lb. tripe or lambs' feet*	2 *quarts water*
1 *medium size onion*	3 *eggs*
Salt	*Juice of two lemons*

Patsas is, strictly speaking, the Turkish name for lambs' feet and tripe is called *skembe*. This soup can be made from either feet or tripe or, if liked, both together. A cowheel would substitute admirably for lambs' feet, with the added advantage of having fewer tiny bones to cope with.

Put the tripe into boiling salted water and simmer for ten minutes without a pan lid, removing any scum which rises to the top. Put in the whole onion and press the tripe down with a plate and cook gently till tender. Remove the tripe from the broth and when cool enough to handle cut into small pieces and put it back into the soup. Beat three eggs with the lemon juice and two tablespoons of cold water. Add two cups of the soup and pour back into the pan away from the fire. If the soup is too thin, thicken with a little cornflour.

TAHINOSOUPA

Tahini is an emulsion made from ground sesame seed. It is rather like a liquid form of peanut butter and tastes very much the same. In Arab countries it is prepared by mixing with water, lemon juice and chopped parsley and is served in a bowl into which you dip pieces of muffin-like bread called *jepates*. I have never found it used in Greece for anything other than this Lenten Soup.

6 oz. Tahini	2 quarts water
Juice of 1 or 2 lemons	Salt
1 cup rice	1 teaspoon tomato paste if liked

Bring the salted water to the boil and throw in the rice. While the rice is cooking mix the *tahini* in a bowl with half a cup of cold water and add the lemon juice. Mix well, then take a ladleful or two of water from the pan and add it to the *tahini* slowly. Pour it all back into the pan away from the fire and serve. A teaspoon of tomato paste may be added but real *tahinosoupa* is served plain.

REVYTHIA   CHICK PEA SOUP

1½ lb. chick peas	1 dessertspoon bicarbonate of
1 or 2 onions	soda
½ pint olive oil	2 quarts water
	Salt

Cover the chick peas with cold water, add a good teaspoon of salt and leave them overnight to soak. Next day, drain away the water and put the chick peas into a colander, having first rubbed them well in the hands with the bicarbonate of soda to loosen the skins. After about one hour put them into a clean kitchen towel and roll them, pressing hard on the table to remove the skins. Rinse well, put them into a pan with two quarts of water and bring to the boil, removing the scum as it rises to the surface. When the water is quite clear add the finely sliced onion, olive oil, pepper, and if necessary, more salt. Simmer gently for about two hours. Serve with lemon juice or wine vinegar.

VI

FISH

Bid them come now, and not delay
Nor vex the cook who's ready for them.
For all the fish is long since boiled,
And all the roast meats long since cold.

Athenaeus

PSARIA FISH

As a country deep in the warmest part of the Mediterranean
mainland, Greece and the islands can draw on a wealth of fish.
To make a broad generalization the most enjoyable food in
both Greek homes and restaurants is likely to be fish or some
other native of the sea. Many varieties of fish find their way
into the Athens market and whereas the average English
housewife is acquainted with about a dozen well-known
varieties her Greek counterpart will be familiar with at least
three dozen apart from the shellfish and cephalopods, i.e.
octopus, squid, etc. The foreigner in Greece is well advised at
first to ask the fishmonger to tell her which should be boiled,
baked or fried.

Red mullet, sole and cod are the leading fish equally
well known in England and in Greece, although the sole
is not treated with quite the same respect as in northern
countries.

The following recipes are particularly Greek and can be
made with great success in England once the prejudice against

66

doing anything with a fish other than boiling, frying or grilling it has been overcome.

Cod, hake, fresh haddock, among the cheaper fish, and halibut, turbot, sea bream or bass among the more expensive or lesser-known fish may be used for any of these dishes. Fish is always sent to the table complete with the head, which is considered the best part.

ACHINOI   SEA URCHINS

Sea urchins are little known in England, but as this is a book on Greek food I have included them. Only the females are edible and they are at their sweetest and best at full moon. Recognizable by their dark purple colour they adorn themselves with tiny pebbles or strands of seaweed and are plumper than the male which is quite black, rather smaller and has longer and sharper spikes. They are not difficult to gather once you have learned to grasp them firmly in the hand and prise them away from the rocks to which they cling. If you should be so unfortunate as to get part of one of the spines in your hand or foot, soak it well in olive oil and remove it with a fine needle, remembering that being very brittle the spikes have to be eased out. They will break if pierced by the needle.

To prepare the sea urchin use a sharply pointed knife or a pair of scissors and cut a large hole in the flat head. Serve in the shell with a squeeze of lemon juice; or carefully remove the coral from the sides with a teaspoon and serve on a small dish with a little lemon juice and olive oil. Mop up the coral with fingers of fresh brown bread.

ASTAKOS   CRAWFISH OR SPINY LOBSTER

Lobsters are rarely found in Greece, although *astakos* is usually referred to as lobster. In reality, they are crawfish (*langouste*) and not to be confused with crayfish (*ecrevisse*), which is a small freshwater shellfish.

Crawfish are quite distinct from lobster which have smooth

shells and large pincer claws. Crawfish on the other hand have no claws but two long antennae and a rough spiny shell. The flesh is a good deal firmer than that of the lobster and in Greece is much preferred, although for my taste they cannot compare with a fresh lobster. To my knowledge, the only parts of Greece where lobsters are to be found are Salonica and Paleocastritsa in Corfu, favourite haunt of Edward Lear, who spent much time there drawing the breathtakingly beautiful coastline. Here you choose your lobster or crawfish alive in the pens and have it cooked while you linger over your *ouzo* or a glass of wine.

Crawfish are usually boiled, cut into slices and served with mayonnaise or with an oil and lemon sauce and garnished with either capers or a sprinkling of *rigani* (*oregano*). They can also be split lengthwise and grilled in the shell over charcoal, when they are delicious but very filling.

BACCALYAROS ME SKORTHALIA
SALT COD WITH GARLIC SAUCE

1 *whole dried salt cod or*	½ *teaspoon baking soda*
6 *fresh cod steaks*	6 *oz. flour*
1 *teaspoon olive oil*	*Water*
Pepper	*Garlic sauce*—skorthalia (*see* 'Sauces')

If dried cod is used, cut the fish into serving portions of about two inches square and soak for twelve hours in cold water, changing the water several times. When ready to cook, drain and dry the pieces of fish. Have ready a fairly thick flour and water batter, seasoned with pepper, and just before using add the olive oil and baking soda. Dip each piece of fish into the batter and fry until crisp and golden in a deep pan of very hot olive oil. Pile on a serving dish and serve with a bowl of *skorthalia*, the famous Greek garlic sauce for which a recipe is given, and a tomato salad garnished with sliced green peppers or a boiled beetroot salad.

Fish

BOURTHETO

BAKED FISH (CORFU)

A variety of fish may be used for this Corfu island speciality. It is a peasant dish and for it the Corfiot buys a couple of kilos of small fish, the cheapest fish in the market. These are a nuisance to eat, being full of tiny bones. Dried cod or a rock fish called *rufios* in Corfu is often used, and are better. Cod steaks, fillets, fresh herring or hake are all equally good.

The success of this dish depends on the amount of cayenne pepper used. The Corfiots just say 'plenty' and, depending on how hot you or your guests can stand it, you must decide for yourself how much to put in.

3 *lb. fish*	2 *tablespoons tomato paste*
½ *pint olive oil*	*Salt*
2 *large onions or*	*Cayenne pepper*
1 *lb. pickling onions*	*Paprika*

Heat the olive oil with a little water in an earthenware casserole and put in the onions. If large onions are used, cut them into quarters and cook slowly and gently until they have softened. Add salt, red pepper to taste and put in the fish. Simmer gently until the fish is cooked. Remove from the fire and stand for at least fifteen minutes before serving.

BARBOUNI

RED MULLET

In Greece red mullet has always been considered a particularly choice fish. While the larger fish are preferred by many and command a high price in the market they have a rather strong flavour which is an acquired taste. The smaller fish are much sweeter and the liver and cheeks are held to be great delicacies. They are usually grilled or fried and served with an olive oil and lemon sauce, but this is the way Crisulla serves them in Spetsai.

Scrape, wash and clean the fish but do not take off the heads nor remove the liver. Dip each fish in seasoned flour and fry in very hot olive oil. Drain and keep hot while the sauce is being made. Add as much flour as will absorb the oil left in the frying-pan after the fish have been cooked. Put in a sprig or two of rosemary, season with salt and pepper and add some wine vinegar, stirring vigorously all the time until the sauce is smooth and the consistency of thick cream. Pour into a warmed sauce boat and serve with the fish.

GARITHES PILAFE   PRAWNS WITH RICE

3 *pints prawns*
1 *small onion*
2 *cloves garlic (if liked)*
2 *oz. butter*
1 *cup tomato pulp*

1 *sprig rosemary or sweet basil*
1 *teaspoon sugar*
½ *wineglass vermouth*
½ *wineglass cream*
A pinch of cinnamon
Salt and pepper

Prepare the prawns as for *garithes vrastes*. Scrape out the heads and keep on one side. Chop the onion and garlic very finely and *sauté* gently in butter until quite soft, then add the scrapings from the prawn heads, the tomato pulp, sugar, cinnamon, rosemary or sweet basil and season with salt and pepper. Simmer slowly for half an hour, remove from the fire and pass through a fine sieve. Return to the pan and put in the prawns with the vermouth and cream and reheat. Have ready a *pilafe*. Press the rice into a ring mould before turning out on to the serving dish. Fill the centre with the prawns and serve hot.

GARITHES VRASTES   BOILED PRAWNS

Prawns have a very delicate flavour which is quite lost if they are merely boiled in a pan of salted water, which they usually are. They should be well washed in several waters to remove any dirt or sand and put into a pan without any water at all. Put a lid on the pan and let them simmer gently in their own liquid over a low flame, shaking the pan from time to time to ensure even cooking. This should take about ten minutes.

Let the prawns cool a little before shelling them. Prepared in this way they retain their full flavour and nothing is lost in the cooking.

Serve them with an olive oil and lemon sauce or a sharp mayonnaise to which have been added a few chopped capers.

GARITHES TIGANITES   FRIED PRAWNS

3 *pints large prawns*	1 *tablespoon olive oil*
4 *oz. flour*	*A pinch of nutmeg*
2 *eggs*	*Salt and black pepper*

If the prawns have been freshly caught they can be shelled easily before cooking. If, however, they have been on ice it is better to prepare them as in the recipe for boiled prawns.

Make a rather thick batter with the flour and egg yolks, thinning down to the required consistency with water. Add the olive oil and seasoning. Beat the egg whites until they form peaks and fold into the batter. Coat each prawn with the batter, drop into a deep pan of very hot olive oil and fry until crisp and golden. Drain on a sheet of greaseproof paper and serve at once with a mayonnaise sauce to which you have added some finely chopped pickled gherkins or capers.

KALAMARAKIA   BABY SQUID OR INKFISH

When they are very tiny and before the inksac has developed, squid are so sweet and tender they can be fried whole.

Wash and drain them well, dust with flour seasoned with salt and pepper and fry in very hot olive oil. They should be crisp and golden brown and served at once with a squeeze of lemon juice. When larger, they may be stuffed with rice and stewed, or cooked in red wine as in the following recipe.

The Greek word for cuttlefish is *soupies*, and it is from the ink of the cuttlefish that the pigment sepia is obtained. The following recipes for squid may also be used for cuttlefish but

Fish

they are not so delicate in flavour and are sometimes a little tough.

KALAMARAKIA ME KRASSI
INKFISH WITH RED WINE

3 *lb. medium size inkfish*
½ *pint olive oil*

1 *wineglass red wine*
1 *teaspoon sugar*

Wash the kalamarakia and remove the small sand sac, leaving the ink inside. Put them into a wide, heavy-bottomed pan without water over a low fire, shaking the pan gently from time to time until the juices have run out and evaporated. Add the olive oil, red wine, sugar and if necessary a pinch of salt and a little water. Cook until tender and leave to cool in the pan.

This dish is eaten cold but not chilled.

KALAMARAKIA YEMISTA
STUFFED INKFISH

2 or 3 *lb. inkfish*
6 *oz. rice*
½ *pint olive oil*
2 *medium size onions*

1 *or 2 ripe tomatoes*
1 *tablespoon finely chopped parsley*
1 *dessertspoon chopped dill*
Salt and pepper

Wash and clean the inkfish, removing both the small sand sac and the ink. The ink may be fried in a little olive oil and served on small squares of brown bread as a delicious *meze*.

Chop the onions finely and *sauté* them in half the olive oil until soft and yellow, then add the rice and when transparent, remove from the fire to cool. Chop the skinned tomato and with the dill and parsley, add it to the rice and onion. Season to taste. Mix in the rest of the olive oil and stuff the inkfish lightly, leaving room for the rice to swell. Tie each one with a piece of thread so that the filling will not come out and pack them closely together in a wide-bottomed pan. Barely cover with water and simmer very slowly until the liquid is nearly all absorbed and the inkfish are tender. This will take about two hours.

OCTAPOTHI ME KRASSI
OCTOPUS COOKED IN WINE

1 *large octopus or 2 small ones*	1 *dessertspoon tomato paste*
½ *pint olive oil*	2 *bay leaves*
1½ *lb. shallots*	2 *gloves garlic*
1½ *lb. new potatoes* (*optional*)	1 *wineglass red wine*
	Salt and pepper

Wash the octopus well, remove the ink and keep on one side. Cut the octopus into pieces about two inches long and put into a pan without water. Leave over a low fire for about twenty minutes until the juices have run out and evaporated, shaking the pan from time to time to avoid burning. Add the olive oil, shallots, bay leaves, garlic and tomato paste diluted with a little water and stir for five minutes. Next put in the wine, the ink from the octopus and enough water just to cover the contents of the pan. Season to taste and cook very slowly for one and a half hours, when the octopus should be tender. Half an hour before serving put in the potatoes and add a little more wine and water if necessary.

OCTAPOTHI PILAFE
OCTOPUS WITH RICE

1 *small octopus*	1 *dessertspoon tomato paste*
1 *finely chopped onion*	6 *oz. rice*
¼ *pint olive oil*	*Salt and pepper*
2 *large ripe tomatoes or*	

Wash the octopus well, remove the ink sac and keep on one side. Cut the octopus into small pieces and put into a pan without water, and leave over a small flame to draw the liquid from the octopus. When the liquid has been re-absorbed add the onion and olive oil and cook gently for ten or fifteen minutes. Next add the chopped and skinned tomatoes or the

73

tomato paste diluted with water and the ink from the octopus. Add enough water to cover and cook until the octopus is quite tender. Throw in the rice and cook rapidly until all the liquid in the pan has been absorbed. Place a dry clean cloth over the pan and leave aside from the fire to draw the steam for ten minutes before serving.

PSARI ME KOLOKYTHIA FISH WITH COURGETTES

1 *whole fish or 6 slices of hake or fresh haddock*	1 *teaspoon chopped parsley*
¼ *pint olive oil*	1 *lb. ripe tomatoes*
3 *medium size onions*	2 *lb. courgettes*
6 *cloves garlic*	1 *teaspoon sugar*
½ *teaspoon chopped dill*	*Pinch of cinnamon*
½ *teaspoon chopped mint*	2 *lemons*
	Salt and pepper

Heat the olive oil in a pan and put in the sliced onion, garlic and herbs. Add the roughly chopped tomatoes, sugar, cinnamon and stir in half a pint of water. Season and simmer for twenty minutes. Scrape the courgettes and if they are more than four inches in length cut them in half. Put them into the pan and lay the fish on top. When the fish is cooked, remove the pan from the fire and squeeze in the lemon juice. Rock the pan from side to side and stand for twenty minutes before serving.

PSARI LEMONATO YIA FOURNO
BAKED FISH WITH LEMON

1 *whole fish weighing 2 to 3 lb.*	3 *garlic cloves sliced*
1 *finely chopped onion*	3 *tablespoons olive oil*
1 *tablespoon chopped parsley*	1 *tablespoon lemon juice*
or	*Salt and pepper to taste*
1 *teaspoon* rigani (*oregano*)	

Prepare the fish for the oven by rubbing it over with salt, pepper and lemon juice and put into an oiled baking-dish.

Spread the onion and garlic on top of the fish, strew with whichever herb you use, pour the olive oil and lemon juice over it and leave to marinate in a cool place for one hour. Bake in a moderate oven for forty-five minutes, basting from time to time.

This dish is equally good without the onion and garlic, which may be rather heavy for some tastes.

PSARI MAYONAISA   FISH MAYONNAISE

Choose a boiling fish weighing between three and four pounds and have it cleaned, remembering not to take off the head. Bring two quarts of water to the boil with a good tablespoon of olive oil, a few celery leaves, two or three small onions, one carrot and season with salt and pepper. Simmer for twenty minutes, then lower the fish gently into the pan and poach it for about half an hour. Draw away from the fire and leave to cool in the water in which it has been cooked. While still warm, take the fish out of the pan and remove the skin and bones and arrange it on a dish for serving. When quite cold cover the fish with a thick mayonnaise and garnish with slices of cucumber, tomato, a few black olives and sliced green peppers.

The liquid in which the fish has been cooked may be set aside and used for *psarosoupa* (fish soup) or *soupa avgolemono* (egg and lemon soup).

PSARI PICTI   JELLIED FISH

Any fish which jells when cooked and left to go cold	1 *tablespoon olive oil*
3 *small onions*	1 *pint water*
3 *or* 4 *celery leaves*	*Juice of* 2 *or* 3 *lemons*
	6 *peppercorns*
	Salt to taste

Put the onions, celery leaves, olive oil and peppercorns into the water and bring to the boil. Add salt and simmer for fifteen minutes. Put in the fish either whole or cut into steaks and poach gently until cooked. Lift the fish out of the pan carefully and put into a deep serving dish. Strain the liquid in the pan, reduce it to about half and pour over the fish. Add the lemon juice, rock the dish once or twice, and leave to jell. Serve very cold.

PSARI PLAKI   STEWED FISH

6 *cod steaks*	1 *teaspoon chopped dill*
2 *large onions*	1 *teaspoon chopped mint*
3 *large ripe tomatoes*	1 *teaspoon chopped celery*
3 *cloves garlic*	*leaves*
½ *pint olive oil*	1 *tablespoon chopped parsley*
½ *pint water*	1 *lemon*
1 *teaspoon sugar*	*Salt and pepper to taste*

Slice the onions finely and colour them lightly in olive oil. Chop the tomatoes roughly and add to the onion with the sliced garlic, herbs, sugar and water and season to taste. Cook until the tomatoes and onion are soft and the liquid has reduced by about one-third, then put in the slices of fish and poach gently. When the fish is cooked take the pan from the fire and squeeze in the juice of one lemon. Rock the pan once or twice to distribute the lemon juice without breaking the fish and stand for thirty minutes. Lift the fish carefully from the pan and arrange on a serving dish. Cover with the contents of the pan and serve hot or cold.

PSARI YIA SKARA   GRILLED FISH

Psari yia skara means, literally, fish grilled over charcoal and there is nothing more delicious than a freshly caught fish cooked in this way. Trout, red mullet, herrings or mackerel are all good for grilling and now that open-air cooking over charcoal is becoming so popular in England, grilled fish makes a welcome change. In Greece a fish that has been grilled over charcoal is always served with olive oil poured over it, a scattering of *rigani* (*oregano*) and garnished with quarters of lemon.

Having cleaned and scaled the fish, rub them over with olive oil before placing them on the grill. See that the charcoal is really glowing and very hot before you start cooking or the fish will stick to the bars and be difficult to lift without breaking.

PSARI SPETSIOTIKO — FISH À LA SPETSAI

Any whole fish or fish steaks may be used. Dried cod may also be used but should be cut into serving portions and soaked well overnight, changing the water at least three times.

3 *lb. white fish*	6 *cloves garlic*
3 *large ripe tomatoes*	1 *teaspoon sugar*
3 *tablespoons olive oil*	*Salt and pepper*
1 *tablespoon chopped parsley*	*Juice of half a lemon*

Skin and chop the tomatoes and put them into a pan with the olive oil and half a cup of water. Add the chopped parsley, sliced garlic and a good teaspoon of sugar. Season to taste and cook for fifteen minutes. Lower the fish carefully into the pan and poach gently in the sauce until the fish is cooked. Allow to stand for half an hour. To serve, put the fish on a large dish and pour the sauce over it. It is equally good eaten hot or cold.

Another method of cooking this dish is to arrange the fish in a well-oiled baking-dish, smother it with the chopped tomatoes, parsley and sliced garlic, add the oil and seasoning and bake in a moderate oven. Serve hot or cold and in either case squeeze the juice of half a lemon over the fish before serving.

PSARI VRASTO — BOILED FISH

Any boiling fish weighing about 3 *lb.*	6 *young carrots*
¼ *pint olive oil*	12 *shallots*
1 *small bunch celery leaves*	12 *small new potatoes*
6 *very small baby marrows*	1 *tablespoon chopped dill*
	Salt and pepper

Wash and prepare the vegetables and put them to boil with two quarts of water in a fish kettle or a pan big enough to take the whole fish. Season to taste and put in the olive oil and dill. When the vegetables are partly cooked, lower the fish into the pan and poach gently. If the vegetables are ready before the fish, lift them from the pan and keep them warm.

Put the fish on a large dish, garnish with the vegetables and serve with an olive oil and lemon sauce (see page 46).

An *avgolemono* soup is usually made from the fish stock and served as a first course.

TARAMA KEFTETHES   FISH ROE RISSOLES

½ *lb. tarama*	*A sprig of dill*
1 *medium size onion*	1 *slice of bread about 3 in.*
3 *cloves garlic*	*thick*
Mint	*Pinch of cinnamon*
Parsley	*Pepper*

Remove the crusts from the bread, soak in water and squeeze dry. Put through a fine mincer with the *tarama*, onion, garlic and herbs, add a pinch of cinnamon, a dash of pepper and mix well together. Leave to stand for two hours. When ready to cook form into small flat cakes, flour well and fry in deep hot olive oil. Serve with a tomato salad.

VII

MEAT

If I but make you now
one forced meat ball, I can in that small thing
give you a specimen of my skill.
And I will serve you up a meal which shall
be redolent of the Athenian breezes.

Athenaeus

A broad experience of meat dishes leaves an impression that they are not among the more imperishable glories of Greece. Then one recalls for instance the fresh-killed baby lamb roasted by the boy Vangeli at the Inn on Mount Helicon, or the young veal at the monasteries of the Meteora, and withdraws from such a drastic generalization.

It is, however, fair to say that the infant sheep and veal are by far the tenderest and most enjoyable of the Greek butcher's wares and for a few months all too fleeting. Lamb is at its best only up to six months old, after this the meat becomes tough and develops a strong flavour rather like goats' meat. This presents the purchaser with an additional hazard, as butchers are sometimes so blind to the sacredness of their calling as to provide the customer with goat at the price of lamb. Veal, too, is killed at an age which might be considered rather adult in northern countries and under the name of *moschari psito*, is a standard dish on the menus of Greek *tavernas*.

The inevitable fact is that Greece is not a great meat-raising country. Apart from a comparatively few areas of good grazing

79

land in the north of Greece, the rest of the country provides
poor fodder for cattle and much has to be imported. The
ingenious Greeks have, over the centuries, learned to make the
best of what they have rather than gloomily accept that the
best is not very good. They eat what might otherwise be
tough and flavourless meat finely minced with a rich anthology
of flavouring.

At Easter, the most important Greek festival, rich and poor
alike feast on Paschal Lamb and only the destitute, of which
there are unfortunately many, are without meat at Easter. On
Maundy Thursday the lamb is killed and hung throughout
Good Friday until Saturday when *mayeritsa*, the Easter Soup,
is prepared from the liver, lungs, heart and entrails of the
young lamb. On Easter Sunday, preparations for the midday
feast begin very early. In the country a shallow trench is dug
and filled with glowing charcoal. A spit, or *souvla* as it is called,
is arranged over the fire and the whole lamb is slowly turned
by hand for several hours and basted from time to time with
lemon juice and olive oil to prevent it from getting too dry.

Greek butchers cut their meat in a unique fashion and one
of the first things the foreign housewife has to learn is that
there are no cheap cuts. Whether you buy a leg of lamb, cut-
lets, or shoulder and neck for stewing you will pay the same
price and probably get a proportion of waste meat with it.
When buying a whole lamb for cooking on the spit or cutting
up at home, the heads and innards, including the liver, will be
weighed in, though it is possible to buy these separately.

Beef and pork are rarely found in the market, although the
traveller will often see a sucking pig being roasted outside a
wayside *taverna* on a Sunday evening during the winter
months when there are no lambs.

ARNI EXOCHICO   LAMB COOKED IN PAPER

There are several methods of cooking *arni exochico*. Some
people cut the lamb into pieces and wrap it in *filo*, the paper-
thin Greek pastry; others take a small leg or shoulder, rub it

well with salt and pepper and after cutting up about half a pound of *fetta* or *kefalotiri* cheese, wrap the whole in several sheets of well-buttered greaseproof paper or tin foil, taking care that no air can get in or out of the parcel. It is then tied up with string and cooked in a medium oven for one or two hours according to the size of the joint. Unwrap the parcel before sending to the table and serve in its own juice.

ARNI FRICASSÉ LAMB FRICASSÉ

Fricassé is a very popular dish in the spring when it is made with Cos lettuce or the fronded variety of endive, also known as chicory. Broad beans left in the pod, artichoke hearts and courgettes, can all be used for this dish and the method of cooking is the same but the meat must be cooked longer before adding these vegetables as they take less time to cook than endive or Cos lettuce and should retain their shape for serving.

3 *lb. stewing lamb*	2 *tablespoons chopped dill*
1 *large bunch spring onions*	1 *teaspoon chopped mint*
4 *heads Cos lettuce or*	*Salt and pepper*
endive	*Egg and lemon sauce (see*
2 *oz. butter*	'Sauces')

Wash and cut the lamb into serving portions. Chop the onions, including the green part, and wash and break the lettuce into pieces as if for salad. Melt the butter in a large saucepan and *sauté* the meat for fifteen minutes before adding the onions, lettuce and herbs. Cook for ten minutes more, then add seasoning. Cover with water and simmer slowly for about one and a half hours until the meat is tender. Make an egg and lemon sauce with the broth and pour back into the pan. Serve hot.

ARNI KAPAMA LAMB RAGOUT

3 *lb. of lamb for stewing*	1 *flat teaspoon sugar*
2 *lb. peeled potatoes*	*Pinch of cinnamon*
1 *lb. ripe or tinned tomatoes*	*Salt and pepper*
	Olive oil

Meat

Trim the meat of as much fat as possible and cut into serving portions. Fry in olive oil to seal the juices and put into a saucepan with the coarsely chopped tomatoes, sugar and cinnamon and season to taste. Barely cover with water and put on the pan lid firmly. Cook slowly for an hour and a half and when the meat is partly cooked put in the potatoes, laying them on top of the meat. If the potatoes are small leave them whole but if they are large, cut into quarters and fry in olive oil before putting them in with the meat to prevent them from disintegrating during cooking. Replace the pan lid very closely and cook until the potatoes are done.

ARNI PSITO   ROAST LAMB

Leg or shoulder of lamb weighing 3 to 4 lb.	½ pint olive oil
	½ pint water
4 cloves garlic or	1 teaspoon rigani (oregano)
4 sprigs rosemary	2 tablespoons lemon juice
6 large potatoes or	Salt and pepper
3 lb. chestnuts	

Prepare the meat for the oven and insert the garlic cloves or sprigs of rosemary under the skin. Rub over with half a lemon, salt, pepper and olive oil. Place the meat in a roasting-tin, surrounded by the potatoes, peeled and cut into quarters. Pour the rest of the olive oil, a cup of water and the lemon juice over the potatoes, season with salt and pepper, and sprinkle liberally with *rigani*. Cook in a hot oven, adding more water if necessary until the meat is ready and the potatoes are nicely browned and have absorbed all the water. Serve with a raw cabbage salad.

If chestnuts are to replace the potatoes the *rigani* and garlic should be omitted and the chestnuts should be parboiled before peeling and putting in with the meat.

Meat

ARNI STO LATHOHARTO   LAMB COOKED IN PAPER

Leg or shoulder of lamb   *Lemon juice*
  weighing 3 to 4 lb.   *Salt and pepper*
2 cloves garlic   *2 sheets greaseproof paper*
Olive oil

Make several deep incisions in the meat and into each stuff
a sliver of garlic. Rub the meat well with salt, pepper, olive
oil and lemon juice. Brush both sheets of greaseproof paper
with olive oil and wrap up the meat, making a neat parcel,
and tie well with string. Put the parcel in a well-oiled roasting-
tin, place in a moderate oven and cook slowly for about two
hours. Cooked in this way, the meat retains all its juices and
flavour and is equally delicious served hot or cold with mashed
potatoes and a salad. If the flavour of garlic is not liked, a
sprig or two of rosemary may be inserted into the meat
instead.

DOLMATHES   STUFFED VINE OR CABBAGE LEAVES

This famous Greek dish has become more or less inter-
nationally known. In Sweden it has been adopted as a national
dish from the time when Charles XII of Sweden, after being
defeated at the battle of Poltana by Peter the Great, spent
some years in Turkey early in the eighteenth century and is
called 'Kåldolma'.

Dolmathes are made with tender young vine leaves or the
inside leaves of a savoy cabbage and are stuffed with meat,
rice and herbs. Vine leaves have a curiously pungent aromatic
flavour and may be obtained in tins when fresh leaves are not
available.

Dolmathes are made with or without meat and may be served
hot or cold. If making without meat, the amount of rice must
be increased to one pound.

3 *to* 4 *doz. vine leaves or*
   1 *Savoy cabbage*
2 *lb. finely minced veal*
6 *or* 8 *spring onions or*
   1 *large onion*
3 *to* 4 *oz. rice*
½ *teaspoon chopped mint*

1 *teaspoon dill or parsley*
Cinnamon
¼ *pint olive oil*
Salt and pepper
Egg and lemon sauce (see
   'Sauces')

Blanch fresh vine or cabbage leaves in boiling water, drain and leave them to cool. Chop the onions finely and mix in a bowl with the meat, rice and herbs. Season with salt, pepper and a pinch of cinnamon. Add the olive oil and work in with the hands. Put one or two leaves, according to size, in the palm of one hand and with the other put a dessertspoon of the filling in the centre of the leaf and make a little parcel by folding the stem over first, then the sides, rolling them as tightly as possible. Pack closely together in a large saucepan. Barely cover with water and press a plate well down on to the *dolmathes* to prevent them unrolling and cook gently for one hour.

Make an egg and lemon sauce with the liquid from the pan and pour back over the *dolmathes*. Shake the pan gently from side to side and stand away from the fire for ten minutes before serving.

DOMATES YEMISTES

TOMATOES STUFFED WITH MEAT

12 *large ripe tomatoes*
2 *lb. finely minced veal*
4 *medium size onions*
½ *pint olive oil*
6 *oz. rice*
Nutmeg

3 *tablespoons chopped parsley*
2 *teaspoons chopped mint*
1 *tablespoon sugar*
2 *tablespoons dried bread-*
   crumbs
Salt and pepper

Slice a piece from the bottom of each tomato and hollow out the pulp and seeds. Sieve the pulp and keep on one side to add to the filling. Arrange the tomatoes in an oiled baking-tin and put a pinch of sugar into each one, leaving them to stand while the filling is being made.

Chop the onions and fry lightly in olive oil. Add the washed rice and cook until transparent before putting in the meat, herbs, a grate of nutmeg and the sieved tomato pulp. Season to taste, stir well and cook slowly for thirty minutes. Remove from the fire and allow to cool. Fill the tomatoes, leaving room for the rice to swell, and replace the caps. Sprinkle with some dried breadcrumbs, moisten with a little olive oil and bake in a fairly hot oven until brown and wrinkled. If available, green peppers are usually stuffed with the same filling and cooked with the tomatoes.

FASSOLIA ME KREAS
MEAT COOKED WITH FRENCH BEANS

3 *lb. veal or lamb for stewing*
4 *ripe tomatoes*
2 *onions*
2 *oz. butter*
3 *tablespoons olive oil*
2 *lb. French beans*
Salt and pepper

Cut the meat into pieces and *sauté* gently in butter. Add the pulped tomatoes, grated or finely chopped onion, olive oil and two cups of hot water and simmer gently for one hour. Put in the sliced beans, season with salt and pepper and cook until the beans soften. Draw aside from the fire and stand for at least twenty minutes before serving to allow the oil to be thoroughly absorbed by the beans.

GIUVETSI   LAMB BAKED WITH NOODLES OR MACARONI

Traditionally, this dish is cooked in a large round shallow earthenware casserole called a *giuvetsi*, hence the name, but it is frequently made in a roasting-tin and the choice is left to the cook. The meat may be left whole or cut into pieces. Any type of macaroni, wide noodles or the square kind called *hilopites* in Greek, may be used.

Meat

3 *lb. shoulder or leg of lamb*	1 *tablespoon lemon juice*
2 *lb. ripe tomatoes*	1 *tablespoon olive oil*
4 *tablespoons butter*	1 *teaspoon sugar*
1 *lb. macaroni, or noodles*	Salt and pepper
or hilopites	1 *pint boiling water*

Rub the meat well with lemon juice, olive oil, salt and pepper, put into a roasting-tin or earthenware casserole with two tablespoons of butter and cook in a moderate oven for about one hour. Make a sauce with the pulped tomatoes, the rest of the butter, sugar and seasoning. Add the water and while the sauce is still bubbling, throw in the macaroni and cook for ten minutes, stirring frequently to keep the pieces from sticking together. If it appears to be too dry, add some tomato juice and more water as the macaroni will absorb the liquid during further cooking in the oven. When the macaroni is partly cooked, put it into the *giuvetsi* with the meat and continue to cook in the oven until a light crust has formed on the macaroni.

KHIRINO ME KITHONIA   PORK WITH QUINCE

3 *lb. pork*	4 *lb. quince*
1 *lb. ripe tomatoes or*	Cinnamon
1 *good teaspoon tomato paste*	Salt and pepper
6 *oz. sugar*	

Cut the meat into serving portions and brown in a little pork fat. Slice the tomatoes and add to the meat. Season with salt, pepper and a pinch of cinnamon. Cover with water and simmer gently about one hour until half cooked. Meanwhile, peel and cut the quince into slices, sprinkle them with sugar and leave on a dish to draw for thirty minutes. Arrange the slices on the meat in the pan and pour in any liquid drawn from the quince. Rock the pan gently and cook about one hour more.

Meat

KEFTETHES

2 lb. minced veal
2 tablespoons grated onion
1 breakfastcup of bread-
  crumbs
2 eggs
2 tablespoons olive oil
1 tablespoon wine vinegar

1 tablespoon finely chopped
  parsley
1 teaspoon chopped mint
½ teaspoon rigani (oregano)
2 cloves garlic (if liked)
2 tablespoons boiling water
Salt and pepper

Put the meat, grated onion and breadcrumbs into a mixing bowl and knead well with the hands. Break in the eggs and continue to knead until the eggs have been well combined. Next mix in the herbs, chopped garlic (if used), olive oil, and moisten with vinegar and hot water. Season to taste and leave for at least one hour before cooking. Shape into balls about the size of a small egg, flour lightly and fry in very hot olive oil until well browned. Drain and serve at once with a boiled or fresh salad.

KEFTETHES ME DOMATA SALTSA
MEAT BALLS WITH TOMATO SAUCE

Prepare the *keftethes* as in the preceding recipe and fry until golden.

For the sauce use fresh ripe tomatoes in the summer, or in winter a tin of whole peeled tomatoes.

Finely slice two or three medium size onions and *sauté* in butter until soft. Chop the peeled tomatoes and add to the onions, season with salt, freshly ground pepper, a teaspoon of sugar and a good pinch of cinnamon. Add a little tomato paste diluted in one cup of water and cook slowly for forty minutes, then put in the *keftethes* and simmer for fifteen minutes more.

Meat

KEFTETHES STO FOURNO · BAKED MEAT BALLS

2 *lb. finely minced veal*
½ *small loaf of dry bread*
1 *cup milk*
4 *oz. dripping or other cooking fat*
1 *tablespoon chopped parsley*

2 *lb. potatoes*
1 *lb. fresh ripe tomatoes or*
1 *tin tomatoes*
1 *cup tomato juice or*
1 *tablespoon tomato paste diluted in water*
Salt and pepper

Cut off the crust and soak the bread in milk seasoned with salt and pepper. Knead into the meat with the parsley and two tablespoons of cooking fat and leave for at least an hour before cooking. Shape into rissoles and place them in a roasting tin with the rest of the cooking fat. Cut the potatoes into quarters and arrange in the roasting-tin with the tomatoes and meat balls. Pour in the tomato juice, reserving a little to moisten during cooking. Cook slowly for one and a half hours in a moderate oven, adding more tomato juice and water if necessary.

Serve with a beetroot salad.

KOLOKYTHIA PAPOUTSAKIA
BABY MARROW WITH MINCED MEAT

1½ *lb. finely minced meat*
3 *tablespoons grated onion*
¼ *pint tomato juice*
¼ *teaspoon cinnamon*
2 *oz. butter*

3 *lb. medium size baby marrows*
1½ *pints Béchamel sauce (see* 'Sauces')
2 *eggs*
2 *oz. grated cheese (Parmesan or kefalotiri)*
Salt and pepper

The word *papoutsakia*, translated literally, means little shoes and this is what baby marrows are supposed to resemble when they are prepared in this way.

Sauté the onion in a little butter, add the minced meat,

seasoned with salt, pepper and cinnamon, and moisten with the tomato juice. Cook slowly for fifteen minutes while you boil the marrows and prepare the Béchamel sauce.

The marrows should be of even size for appearance's sake. Boil them until just cooked in salted water and when cool enough to handle split them lengthwise and hollow out some of the pulp which should be added to the meat filling. Arrange the marrows, split side up, in a well-buttered baking-dish and press a tablespoon of the meat mixture into the hollow of each one. Add the well-beaten eggs and the grated cheese to the Béchamel sauce, which should be rather stiff, and cover each marrow separately. Sprinkle them with more grated cheese and bake in a hot oven until nicely browned.

If the *papoutsakia* are to be served as a first course instead of a main dish the meat filling can be omitted. If preferred, young aubergines, the long variety, may be used for this dish instead of baby marrows.

KOLOKYTHIA YEMISTA ME DOMATES
STUFFED MARROWS WITH TOMATOES

3 *lb. baby marrows*	2 *oz. butter*
2 *lb. minced veal*	2 *tablespoons chopped parsley*
2 *or* 3 *onions*	1 *teaspoon chopped mint*
2 *lb. ripe tomatoes or*	1 *teaspoon sugar*
1 *large tin tomatoes*	*Nutmeg*
2 *oz. rice*	*Salt and pepper*

Prepare the marrows as in the preceding recipe. Chop the onion and *sauté* lightly in the butter. Add the minced meat, herbs, sugar, rice and a grate of nutmeg. Next stir in two tablespoons of the marrow pulp, one-third of the tomato pulp, from which you have sieved the seeds, and if necessary, a little hot water. Season with salt and pepper and cook for fifteen minutes, then draw aside and leave to cool. Fill the marrows to within an inch of the opening to allow room for the rice to swell. Fry them in olive oil, turning frequently until lightly browned and pack them closely together in a large saucepan. Cover with the rest of the tomato pulp and add a teaspoon of tomato paste diluted in hot water if too dry. Simmer gently for one hour.

KOLOKYTHIA YEMISTA ME AVGOLEMONO
STUFFED MARROWS WITH EGG AND LEMON SAUCE

3 *lb. baby marrows*	1 *tablespoon wine vinegar*
2 *lb. minced veal*	1 *tablespoon hot water*
1 *large onion*	*Egg and lemon sauce (see*
2 *tablespoons chopped parsley*	'*Sauces*')
2 *oz. rice*	*Salt and pepper*
1 *tablespoon olive oil*	

Prepare the marrows by cutting a small slice off each end and scoop out the pulp, keeping a little on one side. In Greece a special gadget is used for this purpose but a potato peeler will do just as well. Mix the onion with the minced meat, parsley, rice and about two tablespoons of the marrow pulp. When well combined, add the seasoning and moisten with the olive oil, vinegar and hot water. Fill the marrows, leaving room for the rice to swell during cooking. Pack them closely into a wide saucepan, cover with water and simmer very slowly for one hour. Make an egg and lemon sauce with the liquid from the pan and pour over the stuffed marrows. Serve hot.

KREATOPITTA   MEAT PIE

1½ *lb. minced veal*	*Salt, pepper nutmeg*
2 *medium size onions*	½ *pint Béchamel sauce (see*
2 *tablespoons tomato juice*	'*Sauces*')
2 *oz. butter*	1 *lb.* filo (*pastry sheets*)

Grate the onions as finely as possible and boil for five minutes in a little water to soften. Add the minced meat, tomato juice, butter and seasoning. Stir well and leave to simmer gently for fifteen minutes and mix with the Béchamel sauce. Line a baking-tin with five or six well-oiled pastry sheets. Spread the filling evenly and cover with the remaining pastry sheets, remembering to oil each one as they are smoothed one on another. Fold in the edges to seal in the filling and score the top sheets with a sharp knife. Cover with greaseproof paper and bake in a moderate oven for one hour or until golden and crisp. Cut into squares before serving.

MOSKHARI PSITO   ROAST VEAL

3 *lb. veal for roasting*	1 *onion*
2 *tablespoons cooking butter*	1 *wineglass wine*
Lemon juice	1 *wineglass hot water*
2 *tomatoes*	*Salt and pepper*

Have the meat boned and rolled. Melt the butter in a wide heavy-bottomed saucepan and when very hot, put in the meat previously rubbed over with lemon juice, salt and pepper. Brown well all over, turning frequently. Cut the onion and the tomatoes into quarters and put into the pan with the meat. Add hot water and wine, cover with a lid and cook slowly for two hours, turning the meat from time to time. There should be enough sauce to pour over a dish of spaghetti sprinkled with grated cheese, which is usually served before the meat course. The meat should be sliced before serving with fried potatoes and a salad.

MOUSSAKAS
BAKED AUBERGINES WITH MINCED MEAT AND BÉCHAMEL SAUCE

One of the best known of all Greek dishes, a true *moussaka* is made with the long variety of aubergines but it can also be made with courgettes or potatoes. Made with globe artichokes, it is particularly delicious if somewhat expensive, and takes a long time to prepare if fresh artichokes are used. It can, however, be made with tinned artichoke hearts which make it easier to prepare.

3 or 4 lb. aubergines

2 lb. finely minced veal

2 tablespoons grated onion

2 ripe tomatoes

1 tablespoon chopped parsley

$\frac{1}{4}$ teaspoon cinnamon

$\frac{1}{4}$ teaspoon nutmeg

2 oz. butter

1 wineglass red wine

2 lb. grated cheese (kefalotiri or Parmesan)

1$\frac{1}{2}$ pints Béchamel sauce (see 'Sauces')

3 eggs

Salt and pepper

Olive oil for frying

Slice the aubergines and sprinkle them liberally with kitchen salt, leaving them to drain in a colander for at least thirty minutes to lose the bitterness they would have if this were not done. Rinse well and pat dry with a kitchen cloth. Fry a few slices at a time in hot olive oil until they are nicely browned on both sides. Drain them well and keep warm. In another pan, melt the butter and *sauté* the meat, onions and chopped tomatoes. Add the parsley, spices and seasoning and moisten with the wine and a little water, if necessary. Cook slowly for twenty minutes, then remove from the fire and stir in two tablespoons of the Béchamel sauce. Butter an oblong or square roasting-tin or baking-dish and fill with alternate layers of aubergine and minced meat, sprinkling each layer with a little grated cheese. The bottom and top layers should be of aubergine. Add a grate of nutmeg and the well-beaten eggs to the Béchamel sauce and pour over the dish. Sprinkle with the remainder of the grated cheese and bake in a fairly hot oven for three-quarters of an hour when the top should be golden brown.

MOUSSAKAS ME ANGINARES

MOUSSAKA WITH ARTICHOKES

20 fresh globe artichokes or tinned artichoke hearts

1$\frac{1}{2}$ lb. minced veal

$\frac{1}{2}$ lb. lambs' or calves' brain

2 finely grated onions

2 oz. butter

1$\frac{1}{2}$ pints Béchamel sauce (see 'Sauces')

3 eggs

Salt and pepper

Parmesan cheese

Prepare the artichokes by removing all the tough outer leaves, cut out the choke and use only the hearts. Rub them over with half a lemon, one at a time, and put into a bowl of lemon juice, flour and water to prevent them from going black. Boil until tender, drain and leave to cool. Clean and scald the brain in salted water. Drain, and when cool enough to handle, chop and *sauté* with the meat and onion in butter for ten minutes. Allow to cool a little, then stir in two tablespoons Béchamel sauce and season to taste. Into a well-buttered baking-dish put a layer of sliced artichoke hearts and a layer of meat alternately until the dish is full. Beat the eggs well and fold into the Béchamel sauce before pouring over the contents of the dish. Grate some Parmesan cheese on top and bake in a moderately hot oven for forty-five minutes. Serve with a cucumber and tomato salad.

PASTITSATHA

POT ROAST WITH SPAGHETTI (CORFU)

Pastitsatha is usually made with a boned joint of meat, but it also may be made with steak, which should be cut into serving pieces before cooking.

3 *to* 4 *lb. rolled veal or beef*	1 *stick or* 1 *teaspoon cinnamon*
1 *cup olive oil*	1 *bayleaf*
3 *medium size onions*	2 *cloves*
4 *cloves garlic* (*optional*)	*Salt and pepper*
1 *dessertspoon sugar*	2 *lb. spaghetti*
3 *tablespoons tomato paste*	6 *oz. grated cheese* (*Parmesan or* kefalotiri)

Heat the oil in a heavy pan and brown the roast, turning regularly. Take care to brown well on all sides. Remove from the fire and add the finely chopped onions, garlic, seasoning and spices. Mix the tomato paste with a little hot water before adding to the contents of the pan. Return to the fire, add half a pint of hot water and simmer gently one to two hours according to the size of the joint, until the meat is tender and the liquid reduced to a thick sauce. During cooking it may be necessary to add more hot water from time to time.

Boil the spaghetti (see page 49) and serve either with the meat or as a first course, with the sauce and grated cheese served separately.

PIKTI JELLIED PIG'S HEAD

2 *or* 3 *pig's feet*	*Juice of* 3 *lemons*
1 *small or* ½ *a pig's head*	*Juice of* 2 *oranges*
2 *cloves of garlic* (*if liked*)	1 *bay leaf*
6 *peppercorns*	*Salt and pepper*

Wash and clean the head and feet thoroughly and cover with boiling salted water. Add the peppercorns and bay leaf and simmer gently until the meat begins to fall from the bones. Leave until cool enough to handle, remove all the bones, cut the meat into small pieces and place in a mould. If using garlic, crush well with a pestle and mortar and mix with the lemon juice. Reduce the liquid in the pan, add the orange and lemon juice, pepper and, if necessary, more salt and pour into the mould to cover the meat. Rock once or twice to distribute the liquid and leave to go cold. Turn out of the mould to serve, and decorate with slices of lemon and black olives.

ROULO MEAT ROLL

3 *lb. minced meat*	½ *pint olive oil*
1 *breakfast cup breadcrumbs*	1 *tin tomato juice*
3 *oz. butter*	1 *wineglass red wine*
3 *tablespoons grated onion*	1 *flat dessertspoon sugar*
1 *tablespoon finely chopped parsley*	2 *cloves garlic*
	Salt and pepper
1 *raw egg*	*Flour*
4 *hard-boiled eggs*	

Mix the meat, breadcrumbs, butter and onion together and season with salt and pepper. Add the chopped parsley and

bind with the well-beaten egg and two tablespoons of water.
Spread the meat mixture thickly and evenly on a well-floured
pastry board and place the hard-boiled eggs in a line down the
centre. Fold the meat over the eggs and shape into a roll with
well-floured hands, keeping the outside of the roll liberally
sprinkled with flour or it will stick to the board and be difficult to remove. This is a rather tricky operation and needs
some practice. Heat the olive oil in a pan and when it is
smoking hot, carefully lower the meat roll into it and cook until
golden brown all over, turning from time to time to ensure
cooking. Dilute the tomato juice with wine and half a cup of
water. Add the sugar and garlic cloves and season with salt
and pepper. Pour over the meat and simmer slowly for thirty
minutes, when the sauce should be nearly all absorbed by the
meat. To serve, cut the meat into thick slices and serve hot,
garnished with green peas and fried or mashed potatoes or
noodles.

ROULO ME FILA   MEAT ROLL WRAPPED IN PASTRY

2 lb. minced veal	¾ pint thick Béchamel sauce
1 onion	3 eggs
1 large ripe tomato	1 tablespoon grated cheese (Par-
1 lamb's brain	mesan or kefalotiri)
4 oz. liver	6 or 8 pastry sheets (fila)
4 oz. boiled ham	Butter
3 hard-boiled eggs	½ teaspoon cinnamon
	Salt and pepper

Chop the onion very finely and *sauté* lightly in a little butter.
When soft, add the minced meat and the peeled and chopped
tomato. Season lightly with salt, pepper and cinnamon and
cook slowly for twenty minutes, adding a little water if necessary, but the meat should be rather dry when ready to handle.
Blanch the brain and chop finely with the liver and ham.
Smooth the pastry sheets out and brush each one with melted
butter, laying one on top of another. Spread the meat, leaving

a good margin for folding over, and cover the meat with the brain, ham and liver and, lastly, the sliced hard-boiled eggs. Beat the raw eggs and cheese into the Béchamel sauce and spread over the eggs. Fold in the ends of the pastry sheets, then the sides and roll carefully from end to end. Cover with a piece of greaseproof paper and cook slowly in a buttered baking dish in a moderate oven one hour or until golden brown. Serve with a raw salad.

SOFFRITO STEWED STEAK (CORFU)

A speciality of the island of Corfu and as far as I have been able to discover, unknown in any other part of Greece. *Soffrito* is the Corfiot equivalent of the Lancashire dish, Stewed Steak.

To make it you will require 2 lb. shoulder steak which should be cut into slices about a quarter of an inch thick, then floured and fried in olive oil until well browned on both sides. Barely cover the meat with wine vinegar and a little water. If liked, two or three finely chopped cloves of garlic may be added at this stage. Season well with salt and pepper. Simmer gently until the meat is tender and the liquid reduced to a thick sauce. *Soffrito* should be served with mashed potatoes.

SOUDZOUKAKIA SMYRNA SAUSAGES

2 *lb. minced meat*	2 *lb. ripe or tinned tomatoes or*
1 *cup breadcrumbs*	*tomato juice*
¼ *pint milk*	1 *dessertspoon sugar*
3 *cloves garlic*	2 *bay leaves*
2 *tablespoons grated onion*	*Pinch of cumin*
Flour	1 *small onion*
Salt and pepper	*Olive oil for frying*

Moisten the breadcrumbs with the milk and mix with the minced meat, grated onion and chopped garlic and season with salt and pepper. Shape into fat little sausages about two inches long, roll them in flour and fry in hot olive oil.

Prepare a sauce with the sieved tomatoes or tomato juice, sugar, bay leaves and cumin, season with salt and pepper. Put in the onion, left whole, and simmer the sauce for half an hour. Add the sausages and cook for another fifteen minutes before serving with fried or mashed potatoes and a salad.

SOUVLAKIA — GRILLED MEAT ON SKEWERS

Souvla, the Greek word for a skewer or spit, varies in length from the long metal rod used for roasting a sucking pig or the Easter Lamb, to the small splits of bamboo used to spear tiny morsels of meat when *souvlakia* are served as a *meze*.

The best *souvlakia* I have eaten in Greece are those sold on the landing-stage at Antirhion while waiting for the ferry to cross the Gulf of Corinth from the mainland to the Peloponnese. There, a roaring trade is done by the vendors from half a dozen little covered stalls each equipped with a small charcoal grill, a pile of *souvlakia* marinaded in lemon juice and olive oil and a stock of fresh, crusty loaves cut into thick chunks, ready to provide the hungry traveller with the most delicious sandwich ever, for the princely sum of fourpence halfpenny each.

For a main meal, a metal skewer about twelve inches long, having a small ring at one end and a flat point at the other for spearing the meat, is used for this simple but very Greek method of cooking meat. Grilled very quickly over a red-hot charcoal fire, *souvlakia* must be eaten the minute they are ready, otherwise the meat becomes tough and leathery.

2 *lb. lean lamb, veal or pork fillet*	1 *flat teaspoon* rigani *(oregano)*
2 *tablespoons olive oil*	12 *bay leaves*
Juice of half a lemon	*Salt and pepper*

Allowing one skewer for each person, cut the meat into small pieces the size of a walnut and thread on to the skewers with bits of bay leaf in between. Leave about an inch of space at either end of the skewers for them to rest on the grill. Beat

Meta

the lemon juice into the olive oil, season with salt, pepper and *rigani* and leave the *souvlakia* to marinade for half an hour. Grill over a very hot fire, turning constantly, so that the meat becomes well seared on the outside and tender and juicy inside. Serve straight from the fire with a tomato and cucumber salad and quarters of lemon to squeeze over the meat.

STIFATHO   CASSEROLE OF MEAT OR HARE

This is a very rich and popular winter dish and is made with veal, beef or hare. It may be cooked in a saucepan but it is better if an earthenware casserole is used.

3 lb. stewing steak or hare	½ wineglass wine vinegar
3 lb. shallots or pickling onions	4 cloves garlic
½ pint olive oil	2 bay leaves
3 ripe tomatoes or	1 small cinnamon stick
1 dessertspoon tomato paste	A pinch of cumin
1 wineglass red wine	Salt and pepper

Cut the meat or hare into serving portions and brown lightly in half the olive oil before putting into the earthenware casserole. Barely cover with hot water and stew gently for one hour. Reduce the tomatoes to a *purée* and with the whole onions, garlic, bay leaves, spices, red wine, wine vinegar and the remainder of the oil, add to the meat. Stir once with a wooden spoon, cover with a lid and cook very slowly for a further two hours, rocking the casserole now and then instead of stirring, as the onions should remain whole. Allow to stand for a little while before serving.

TAS KEBAB   MEAT WITH PILAFE

2 lb. veal or stewing steak	1 wineglass vermouth
2 oz. butter	1 pint hot water
2 finely sliced onions	1 teaspoon sugar
4 very ripe tomatoes	Pinch of cinnamon
1 good teaspoon tomato paste	Salt and pepper

98

Melt the onions in the butter, using a heavy saucepan. Add the skinned and pulped tomatoes, cinnamon, sugar and the tomato paste diluted in water. Season with salt and pepper. Cut the meat into small pieces and put into the pan. Stir in the water, cover the pan and cook very slowly for one hour or until the meat is tender. Just before serving, stir in a wineglass of vermouth. Serve with a pilafe.

If liked, the rice may be cooked with the meat. In this case more water must be added before throwing in the rice.

YOUVARLAKIA   MINCED MEAT AND RICE BALLS

2 *lb. finely minced meat*	3 *oz. rice*
2 *large grated onions*	1 *tablespoon wine vinegar*
3 *tablespoons chopped parsley*	¼ *pint hot water*
1 *teaspoon chopped mint*	*Salt and pepper*
2 *oz. butter*	*Egg and lemon sauce (see 'Sauces')*

Put the minced meat, onion, parsley, mint and half the butter into a mixing bowl and knead until well blended. Scald the rice for five minutes, then knead into the mixture. Moisten with vinegar and hot water, add the seasoning and leave in a cool place for thirty minutes or more. Shape into round balls the size of a small egg and arrange them in rows in a wide-bottomed saucepan. Barely cover with boiling water, pouring it in carefully from the side so as not to break the meat balls. Add salt and the rest of the butter and press down with a plate before putting on the pan lid. Simmer for three-quarters of an hour. Make an egg and lemon sauce with the broth from the pan, pour over the meat balls and serve without further cooking.

VIII

POULTRY AND GAME

Then let us have a cock, a tender pigeon,
A partridge, and a few such other things;
And if a hare should offer, then secure it.

Athenaeus

———————————

Greece seems at times, particularly in early September, to be a posting-stage for all the migrating birds of the world. Clouds of birds, big and dense enough to blacken the sky, settle to rest in the hillsides before taking off on the final hop of their journey south.

This first migration brings out the 'hunters' and the stillness is constantly shattered by the bark of the numerous guns in search of *ortikia* (quail). Later in the month come the *trigonia* (turtle dove) and last of all, when the weather gets colder, *becatses* (French woodcock) and *perthikes* (partridge). These last are rock partridge and rather tough and uninteresting to eat unless cooked for a long time in a good rich sauce.

Pigeon is a popular table bird and wild duck is regarded as a great delicacy by those 'hunters' who spend their winter weekends in the marshes of Messolonghi and by the lakes of Macedonia. There is no special way of cooking them. They can be pot roasted or casseroled but an essential part of the preparation of wild duck is to sear the inside of the bird with a red-hot poker or a glowing piece of charcoal to eliminate the fishy taste which it would have if this were not done, since wild duck feed mainly on fish. The liver should be thrown away at once.

If the duck is to be kept a while, the inside may be seared and packed with salt and bay leaves or rosemary until the time of cooking.

BECATSA ME KRASSI WOODCOCK WITH WINE

6 *woodcock*
1 *onion*
4 *oz. butter*
1 *tablespoon olive oil*

¼ *pint water*
1 *wineglass red wine*
Salt and pepper

Clean and truss the birds and put them into a deep earthenware casserole. Add the finely chopped onion, butter, olive oil, water and red wine. Season to taste and cover with a lid. Cook in a moderate oven and baste frequently. Quail may be cooked in the same way but wrap each bird in a strip of streaky bacon first as they are rather dry little birds.

GALOPOULO TURKEY

From about November onwards turkeys are to be seen strung out by the hundred in the butchers' shops and are not reserved exclusively for Christmas or New Year as in England. However, now that foreigners have imposed that Nordic commercial traveller, Santa Claus, on the Greeks and that Christian celebrations have been added to New Year's, turkeys disappear about two weeks before Christmas but return by thousands around Christmas Eve. Very often a turkey is pot roasted without stuffing, but if stuffing is used, the most popular are a chestnut stuffing or one made with minced meat.

CHESTNUT STUFFING

For a turkey weighing between seven and nine pounds you will need:

1½ *lb. chestnuts*	*Cinnamon*
1 *onion*	3 *oz. pine nuts*
1 *lb. minced veal*	3 *oz. currants or sultanas*
¼ *pint tomato juice*	*Salt and pepper*
1 *tablespoon sugar*	

Boil and peel the chestnuts, leaving them whole. Slice the onion finely and *sauté* lightly in a little butter until soft but not coloured, then add the minced meat and cook for a few minutes until the meat has lost its raw look. Add the tomato juice, sugar, salt, pepper and a pinch of cinnamon. Stir for a few minutes over a low fire and mix in the chestnuts, pine nuts and sultanas. Leave to cool awhile before stuffing the bird, which may then be roasted in the usual way.

MINCED MEAT STUFFING

¾ *lb. calf's liver*	1 *tablespoon chopped parsley*
Turkey giblets	1 *tablespoon sugar*
1 *lb. minced veal*	¼ *pint tomato juice*
1 *onion*	*Salt and pepper*

Put the liver and giblets into a small pan with enough water to cover them and simmer gently for fifteen minutes and allow to cool. Keep the giblet stock on one side for making a gravy. Cut up the liver and giblets finely and mix together with the minced veal, chopped onion and parsley. Add the sugar, season to taste and moisten with the tomato juice. Stuff the bird and roast in the usual way.

RICE STUFFING

Another good turkey stuffing is prepared by boiling a coffee cup of rice in the giblet stock for about five minutes. Cut up the cooked giblets and add to the rice with one tablespoon of grated cheese, *kefalotiri, kasseri* or Parmesan, one dessertspoon chopped walnuts or pine kernels, a generous knob of butter and, if necessary, a little water. Season with pepper and salt and cook until the liquid has disappeared. Allow to cool before stuffing the bird.

This also makes a good stuffing for chicken.

KOTOPOULO YEMISTO STUFFED CHICKEN

This is Crisulla's recipe for stuffed chicken, although chicken is rarely served this way in Greece. Usually they are boiled and the broth used for *avgolemono soupa* or they are pot roasted in butter; but the most usual method of cooking a chicken is on the spit and the traveller in Greece will find many *tavernas* throughout the country with a small boy standing patiently turning the spit threaded with half a dozen chickens.

1 *large or two small chickens*	*Chicken giblets*
1 *cup diced white bread*	*Rigani (oregano)*
1 *cup finely chopped onion*	*Salt and pepper*
6 *slices bacon*	

Singe and wash the chicken and prepare the stuffing. Chop up the giblets with three slices of bacon and mix together with the finely chopped onion and diced bread. Add seasoning and a pinch of *rigani*.

Stuff the bird with this dry stuffing. Butter it well on the outside and roast in the oven. Twenty minutes before removing from the oven, cover the breast with the rest of the bacon.

KOTOPITTA CHICKEN PIE

1 *chicken*	2 *tablespoons grated cheese*
4 *oz. butter*	(kefalotiri *or Parmesan*)
3 *tablespoons flour*	*Salt, pepper*
3 *eggs*	*Nutmeg*
	12 *oz.* filo (*pastry sheets*)

Cover the chicken with cold water, season with salt and bring to the boil. Remove any scum that rises to the surface and simmer gently until cooked. Leave the bird in the broth, and when cool enough to handle, remove the meat from the bones and flake it finely with the fingers, discarding the skin and any hard pieces.

Make a sauce with two ounces of butter, flour and the chicken broth. Add the well-beaten eggs and grated cheese and pour over the chicken. Season to taste.

Line a shallow baking-tin with half the *filo*, brushing each sheet with melted butter. Spread the filling evenly and cover with the remaining buttered pastry sheets. Fold in the ends neatly to seal in the filling and brush the top sheet liberally with butter. Score into squares with a sharp knife, cover with greaseproof paper and bake in a moderate oven for one hour or until golden and crisp.

Cut into squares before serving.

ORTIKIA   QUAIL

One method of cooking quail is to make a mud dough of red earth and rainwater, wrap the plucked birds in it and cook them in a primitive oven until the mud has baked hard and dry, when the quail will be soft and tender.

Another way is to scoop out the flesh of an aubergine and put the cleaned bird inside, baking it in a slow oven until the aubergine is soft and wrinkled. If neither of these appeal then try one of the following recipes.

ORTIKIA PILAFE   QUAIL WITH RICE

6 *or* 8 *quail*	1 *wineglass of red or white wine*
1 *tablespoon olive oil*	$\frac{1}{4}$ *pint water*
2 *oz. butter*	*Boiled rice*
	Salt and pepper

Put the birds into a shallow earthenware dish with the olive oil, butter, wine and water, season to taste and cover with a close-fitting lid. Cook slowly in a moderate oven until tender. When ready to serve, arrange them on a bed of rice and pour over the juices left in the baking-dish.

Poultry and Game

ORTIKIA SKARAS GRILLED QUAIL

Cut the birds in two, rub each half with salt and pepper and roll them in olive oil and *rigani* (*oreganum*). Leave them to marinade for thirty minutes, turning frequently. Cook them over a charcoal fire or under the grill.

ORTIKIA YIA SOUVLA QUAIL ON THE SPIT

Thread the birds on to a spit and cook them over a hot charcoal fire, turning slowly all the time. Brush them frequently with olive oil and lemon juice to keep them moist.

IX

VEGETABLE DISHES

But often taste your dishes
while you are boiling them. Do they want salt?
Add some: is any other seasoning needed?
Add it and taste again till you've arrived
at harmony of flavour, like a man
who tunes a lyre till it rightly sounds.

Athenaeus

Whereas in England vegetables are apt to be thought of as 'veg', one of the few diminutives with a dense atmosphere of gloom, in Greece they are regarded as a positive pleasure, with an important and leading role in the meal. They are nearly always eaten as a salad, either raw or boiled, and allowed to cool and served with an oil and lemon, or oil and wine vinegar dressing, or they can form the basis of a main dish.

A wide variety of vegetables is grown in Greece, but, like the fruits, they mainly have a short season and for some such as peas, broad beans and artichokes it is very short indeed. In the winter months, Savoy cabbages, cauliflowers and broccoli are at their cheapest and best and are served daily as a salad at the table of every Greek family. These are followed by Cos lettuce which, it is said, originated on the Island of Cos in the Dodecanese. The Greek word for this type of lettuce is *marouli*, while all other varieties are known simply as *salata*.

The most typically Greek approach to vegetables is in the use of the various varieties of spinach and wild greenstuffs known to the Greeks as *horta* and to the British largely as weeds. These grow well after the autumn rains and continue through the winter and short spring until early summer, after which a shortage of water makes them very scarce and raw salads are confined to cucumbers and tomatoes. The term *horta* covers both cultivated and wild greens, many of which are to be found growing prolifically in the English countryside. At the age of seven my small daughter, having lived in Greece all her life, could take me through the fields in England and tell me which of the different *horta*, when boiled, would be sweet or bitter.

Dandelion leaves, in Greek *radikia*, are most popular and several varieties are cultivated and sold in the market, although the wild varieties are considered to be the greater delicacy. The yellow-flowering weed known as charlock or mustard, the farmer's bane in an English cornfield, is a special delicacy called *vrouva*. I remember a Greek friend of mine, seeing a field full of charlock in Sussex for the first time, exclaiming: 'The farmer would have no need to complain of a ruined crop if this were in Greece. All the *vrouva* would have been gathered by Greek women long before it flowered!'

Because of the lushness of the English countryside these wild delicacies, *radikia*, *vrouves* and wild asparagus are bigger and finer in flavour than those found in Greece. They should, of course, be gathered when they are young and tender and before they flower. In the spring and early summer most English gardens will provide a nice boiling of dandelion leaves which, eaten cold with a dressing of olive oil and lemon juice, is a delicious addition to a meal.

Of the root vegetables grown in Greece beetroot, carrots and potatoes are found in the market all the year round. Beetroot is gathered very young and served together with the leaves, which have been boiled separately, and dressed with olive oil and wine vinegar.

Around Christmas and with the coming of the early lamb, Cos lettuce and endive are cheap in the market, followed by globe artichokes, which can be seen growing by the acre in the market gardens around Athens. These, too, are very cheap in the spring as are broad beans, runner beans and peas. In the summer months aubergines (egg plant), courgettes (baby marrow) and okra (ladies' fingers), green peppers, tomatoes and cucumbers provide a variety of cooked dishes and salads.

In Greece, most of the vegetable dishes cooked in olive oil are eaten tepid or cold and are called *lathero fayi*. Tepid food is an acquired taste, but, in any case, such dishes must always stand for some time after they are cooked or the oil and water will not combine well, but remain separate.

ANGINARES ME KOUKIA
ARTICHOKES WITH BROAD BEANS

Of the several varieties of artichokes grown in Greece the most popular is the small global variety which has a more delicate flavour and a smaller choke than the larger kind usually served in France à *la vinaigrette*. The Jerusalem or root artichoke is not known in the Greek kitchen.

12 *globe artichokes*	1 *teaspoon chopped mint*
1½ *lb. shelled broad beans*	1 *breakfast cup olive oil*
1 *large bunch spring onions*	1 *tablespoon lemon juice*
2 *or* 3 *tablespoons chopped dill or fennel*	*Salt and pepper*

To prepare the artichokes remove all the tough outer leaves and slice off the tops of the inner leaves. Trim with a sharp knife, leaving about an inch of stem on each artichoke. When young and tender the hairy choke, being undeveloped, need not be removed. As each artichoke is prepared it should be rubbed over with half a lemon and thrown quickly into a bowl of water in which has been mixed two tablespoons of flour, some kitchen salt and the juice of a lemon. This is done to prevent the artichokes from discolouring.

Put the beans, chopped onions and herbs into a wide, shallow pan with the olive oil and *sauté* them gently for about ten minutes. Arrange the artichokes with the heads down, on the contents of the pan, season to taste, add the lemon juice and barely cover with water. Cut a round of greaseproof paper to fit the pan and press it gently down on the artichokes with a plate. Simmer very slowly for about one hour and leave to stand for at least half an hour before serving.

If the beans are very young and fresh from the garden they need not be shelled. Trim and wash them and put into the pan whole.

This dish is equally good if garden peas are used instead of broad beans in which case add one teaspoon of sugar and, if liked, a chopped ripe tomato.

ANGINARES ALA POLITA   ARTICHOKES IN OIL

12 *globe artichokes*	½ *pint olive oil*
12 *shallots*	2 *tablespoons chopped dill or*
12 *small new potatoes*	*fennel*
12 *young carrots*	*Salt and pepper*
	1 *pint water*

Prepare the artichokes as in the preceding recipe.

Put the shallots into a large saucepan with a pint or more of water and bring to the boil. Add the olive oil and season with salt and pepper. Next put in the potatoes, then the carrots and lastly the artichokes, one at a time with their heads down and, if necessary, add a little more water as the artichokes should be just covered. Cut a piece of greaseproof paper to fit the saucepan, make a hole in the middle to let the steam escape and place it over the artichokes before putting on the lid. This is done to keep them a good colour. After about ten minutes sprinkle in the dill and cook until the artichokes are tender. This should take about an hour. Remove the artichokes with care and arrange them on a serving dish. Garnish with the shallots, potatoes and carrots.

To thicken the sauce, mix a teaspoon of cornflour and a teaspoon of flour with a little water and add to the contents of the pan. Rock the pan gently and cook five minutes more, pour the sauce over the artichokes and leave to cool.

Vegetable Dishes

This dish makes a perfect first course to a meal and should be eaten cold but not chilled.

BAMYES

2 lb. ladies' fingers
3 onions
1 lb. tomatoes
½ pint olive oil

1 dessertspoon sugar
1 dessertspoon wine vinegar
Salt and pepper

Trim the tops of the ladies' fingers, wash them and spread them out on a large dish. Sprinkle them with salt and leave in the sun for an hour to draw off the slime. Slice the onions and tomatoes and cook them gently in olive oil and half a cup of water for one hour.

Lower the ladies' fingers into the sauce. Add pepper, sugar and vinegar. Shake the pan gently and bring slowly to boiling point. Cook slowly for about one hour, then draw the pan away from the fire and stand for half an hour before serving.

This dish may be eaten tepid or quite cold.

DOLMATHES (Crisulla's recipe)

STUFFED VINE LEAVES

25 young and tender vine leaves or the tinned variety
4 oz. rice
½ pint olive oil

1 teaspoon dill or fennel
Bunch of spring onions
1 teaspoon chopped mint
½ pint boiling water
Salt and pepper

If using fresh vine leaves first blanch them in boiling water, drain and cool. Cook the rice in half a pint of boiling water for five minutes. Add the olive oil, chopped herbs, seasoning and chopped onions and mix them all well together. Cook over a low flame for ten minutes, stirring from time to time. Allow the mixture to cool a little then put a vine leaf on the palm of one hand and with the other put a heaped teaspoon of the filling in the centre of the vine leaf. Starting at the stem end of the vine leaf, roll it tightly, turning in the sides and ends to make a little parcel so that the filling will not come out. Do this with each vine leaf, using all the filling. Pack the *dolmathes* into a pan, layer on layer, and barely cover with water. Cook slowly with a plate pressed well down to prevent the *dolmathes* from breaking up in cooking.

Simmer for about one hour and serve either hot or cold with *yaourti* (yoghourt) or an egg and lemon sauce.

If required for *mezes* make them as small as possible and leave them to go cold in the pan.

DOMATES ME MAYONAISA
TOMATOES WITH MAYONNAISE

6 *large firm tomatoes*	1 *tablespoon sugar*
2 *lb. potatoes*	*Mayonnaise*
1 *onion or a few spring onions*	6 *hard-boiled eggs*
2 *tablespoons wine vinegar*	2 *tins sardines*
2 *tablespoons olive oil*	1 *tin anchovies*
½ *teaspoon mustard*	*Olives*
Salt	*A few capers*
	Chopped parsley to garnish

Boil the potatoes in their skins and when cool enough to handle, peel and cut into small cubes. Chop the onion finely, mix the mustard and salt with the olive oil and vinegar and pour over the onion and potato. Turn well and leave to marinade for half an hour. Cut a slice from the bottom of the tomatoes, remove about a dessertspoonful of the pulp and sprinkle a little sugar inside each one. Mix three tablespoons of mayonnaise with the potato and onion and fill the tomatoes. Pile the rest of the diced potato in the centre of the dish, arrange the tomatoes round the potatoes and garnish with hard-boiled eggs cut in halves, sardines, anchovies, olives, capers and mayonnaise. Sprinkle with finely chopped hard-boiled egg and parsley and serve chilled.

DOMATES YEMISTES HORIS KREAS

STUFFED TOMATOES

12 *large ripe tomatoes*	3 *to* 4 *oz. currants*
1 *lb. onions*	1 *tablespoon sugar*
½ *pint olive oil*	½ *teaspoon cinnamon*
1 *tablespoon chopped parsley*	*Dried breadcrumbs*
1 *teaspoon chopped mint*	*Salt and pepper*
12 *oz. rice*	

Prepare the tomatoes by turning them upside down and cutting a little cap from the bottom. Scoop out the pulp and seed and throw the seeds away but keeping the pulp on one side. Fry the onion, mint and parsley together in olive oil until the onions are soft but not coloured. Add the washed rice, tomato pulp, seasoning and a little water, if too thick. Cook for five minutes, then add the currants and sugar and cook for ten minutes more. Draw away from the fire and leave to cool.

Put a pinch of sugar in each tomato before the filling, leaving room for the rice to swell. Replace the caps and sprinkle with dried breadcrumbs. Pour a little oil over each tomato and bake in a moderate oven until brown. If available, a few green peppers can be prepared in the same way and baked with the tomatoes.

FASSOLIA YIACHNI

BEAN AND TOMATO STEW

2 *lb. runner beans*	½ *pint hot water*
1 *lb. ripe tomatoes*	1 *tablespoon sugar*
3 *or* 4 *onions*	*Salt and pepper*
½ *pint olive oil*	

String and slice the beans or, if fresh from the garden, break them in two halves, peel and chop the tomatoes and grate the onion. Heat the oil in a large pan, put in the onions and tomatoes and cook them gently until soft, then add the beans, seasoning and hot water. Simmer until tender, then draw away from the fire and stand for about half an hour before serving. Serve warm or cold.

Vegetable Dishes

If the dish is to be served as a main course, it will be rather more substantial if a few small potatoes are peeled and cooked on top of the beans.

IMAM BAYALDI STUFFED AUBERGINES

Many are the stories about the origin of this dish but the following is the one I like best.

During the Turkish occupation of Greece, a certain Pasha invited an 'Imam', an official of the mosque, to lunch with him. The Imam, noted for his gluttony, was suffering from a jaded appetite and the Pasha, wishing to impress his guest, commanded his cook to think of something different to tempt him. The poor man racked his brains and was almost in despair when the kitchen boy came from the market with a basket of beautiful dark, shiny, purple aubergines. The cook prepared them as they had never been prepared before and the Imam found them so good he ate and ate until he swooned away, which in Turkish is to *bayaldi*. The long variety of aubergine is always used for this dish.

2 *lb. small aubergines*	4 *cloves garlic*
½ *pint olive oil*	1 *tablespoon chopped parsley*
6 *ripe tomatoes*	1 *teaspoon sugar*
4 *onions*	*Salt and pepper*

Wash and trim the aubergines. Make a slit in the sides and remove the seeds and some of the pulp. Keep the pulp on one side. Sprinkle the inside with salt and stand for thirty minutes. Next fry them lightly in hot olive oil and put them on one side to drain while you prepare the filling. Chop the tomatoes, onion and garlic and mix with the aubergine pulp, chopped parsley, sugar and seasoning and fry lightly. When cool enough to handle, stuff the aubergines and pack them into a wide-bottomed pan if they are to be cooked on top of the stove, or a baking-dish if they are to be cooked in the oven. They are equally good either way. Pour in any oil left over from frying the aubergines and cook for three-quarters of an hour. Leave to cool before serving.

Delicious as it is, this dish may be too heavy and oily for some, in which case cook the stuffing in a little water instead of olive oil and do not fry the aubergines before stuffing.

KOLOKYTHIA COURGETTE OR BABY MARROW

The well-known large English marrow is never found in Greece. Baby marrows called *kolokythia* in Greece, courgettes in France and zucchini in Italy, are found in abundance and provide a variety of dishes for the greater part of the year. They are chosen for their size according to the recipe to be followed. Tiny and still bearing the flower, for salads and *soufflés*; a little larger, for *moussaka* and *papoutsakia*, and about six inches in length, for stuffed marrows.

Baby marrows will grow prolifically in England and I have grown them very successfully myself in my own garden. One summer, after giving some seeds to a friend during his visit to Greece, I received a panic letter asking me to send him some more recipes as his own garden in Essex and the kitchen garden at Balliol College, Oxford, were in danger of being overrun by *kolokythia* and no one knew what to do with them apart from boiling them.

KOLOKYTHIA KEFTETHES MARROW RISSOLES

2 *cups marrow pulp*
3 *boiled potatoes*
2 *onions*
1 *slice stale bread about one inch thick*

1 *cup grated cheese (Parmesan or* kefalotiri)
½ *teaspoon chopped mint*
1 *dessertspoon chopped parsley*
Salt and pepper

Cut the crust from the bread, soak in a little water and squeeze dry. Mince all the ingredients very finely and add the grated cheese and beaten egg. Mix well together, then, taking a spoonful of the mixture at a time, form into little flat cakes with floured hands. Fry in hot olive oil until golden. Drain, and serve hot and crisp with a tomato salad. They make an excellent supper dish and are very popular with children.

KOLOKYTHO-KORFATHES
STUFFED COURGETTES FLOWERS

This rather exotic-sounding dish can only be made when the flowers are gathered fresh from the garden and used at once. They are so delicate they fade very quickly.

25 courgette flowers
6 spring onions (12 if very young)
¼ pint olive oil
6 oz. rice
1 good teaspoon tomato paste
1 tablespoon chopped parsley
1 teaspoon chopped dill or fennel
1 teaspoon chopped mint
1 teaspoon sugar
Pinch of cinnamon
1 clove garlic
Salt and pepper

Chop the onions and garlic and fry lightly in olive oil until soft. Wash and add the rice and the tomato paste diluted in a little water and cook for five minutes more, then mix in the herbs, sugar, cinnamon and season to taste. Fill each flower carefully, folding in the petals to keep the filling in, and pack tightly in a large saucepan. Barely cover with water and cook gently for twenty minutes, then draw away from the fire and stand a while before serving.

Make an egg and lemon sauce with the liquid from the pan, pour over and serve. If preferred, they may be cooked in a tomato sauce and minced meat may be added to the filling, in which case reduce the amount of rice by half and do not cook the filling before stuffing the flowers. They will, of course, then take one hour to cook instead of twenty minutes.

Vegetable Dishes

KOLOKYTHIA PAPOUTSAKIA HORIS KREAS
LITTLE SHOES WITHOUT MEAT

2 lb. medium size marrows (courgettes)
3 onions
1 tablespoon chopped parsley
2 oz. butter
3 oz. breadcrumbs
6 oz. grated cheese (Parmesan or kefalotiri)
3 eggs
1 pint Béchamel sauce (see 'Sauces')
Salt and pepper

Chop the onions and cook them gently in very little water until soft. Add butter, parsley, cheese, breadcrumbs and two well-beaten eggs. Mix together and season to taste.

Top and tail the marrows and cook them in boiling salted water for ten minutes, then remove from the fire to cool and drain. Split them lengthwise and remove a little of the pulp from the centre of each half, making them resemble little boats. Put a spoonful of the onion mixture in the hollow of each one and arrange them in a well-greased baking-dish. Cover with a thick Béchamel sauce into which you have beaten an egg. Sprinkle with a little grated cheese and bake in a hot oven until golden.

KOLOKYTHIA SOUFFLÉ   MARROW SOUFFLÉ

I have given three recipes for *kolokythia soufflé*. The first is a simple country one where such refinements as special *soufflé* dishes, regulated ovens and kitchen scales are unknown. The second is a more sophisticated one I have often eaten in Athens and the third uses up the pulp left over from preparing stuffed marrows.

KOLOKYTHIA SOUFFLÉ (1)   MARROW SOUFFLÉ

2 lb. marrows (courgettes)
3 eggs
6 oz. grated cheese (kefalo-tiri, kasseri or Parmesan)
4 oz. butter
Nutmeg
Salt and pepper

Scrape and slice the marrows and boil them in salted water until tender. Mash them in a colander and leave to drain for about one hour.

Mix in the butter, grated cheese and the egg yolks. Season with pepper and a grate of nutmeg. Beat the egg whites separately and fold into the mixture. Pour into a well-buttered dish, sprinkle the top with a little grated cheese and brown in the oven.

KOLOKYTHIA SOUFFLÉ (2)   MARROW SOUFFLÉ

1 *lb. young marrows*	4 *eggs*
4 *oz. butter*	4 *oz. grated cheese* (*Parmesan,*
3 *tablespoons flour*	*kefalotiri or* kasseri)
1 *pint milk*	*Nutmeg*
	Salt and pepper

Prepare a basic *soufflé* mixture with the flour, cheese, butter, egg yolks and milk. Season with salt, pepper and a grate of nutmeg.

Boil some small young marrows until tender but not too soft. Cut them into slices about half an inch thick and put them into the sauce. Fold in the egg whites carefully and pour into a *soufflé* dish. Sprinkle with grated cheese and cook in a fast oven till golden and well risen. Serve immediately. Keep the guests waiting, not the *soufflé*.

KOLOKYTHIA SOUFFLÉ (3)   MARROW SOUFFLÉ

4 *oz. butter*	6 *eggs*
3 *tablespoons flour*	2 *cups marrow pulp*
4 *oz. grated cheese* (*Parme-*	*Nutmeg*
san or kefalotiri)	*Salt and pepper*
1 *pint milk*	

Melt the butter in a thick-bottomed pan, add the flour, stir and cook gently. Add the cheese and warmed milk slowly, keeping a little cheese aside for the top. Separate the eggs and stir in the yolks away from the fire and cool. Sieve the marrow pulp and add to the sauce. Season to taste with a dash of salt, a grind of pepper and pinch of nutmeg. Mix together and fold in the well-beaten egg white very lightly. Pour into a buttered *soufflé* dish, sprinkle with grated cheese and cook in a fast oven until golden and well risen. Serve immediately and remember that a *soufflé* waits for no man.

KOLOKYTHIA TIGANITA

FRIED COURGETTES

Slice some fairly large courgettes into rounds about a quarter of an inch thick. Make a thick batter with a well-beaten egg, a tablespoon and a half of flour, a pinch of baking soda, salt, a grind of black pepper and a little water. Dip the sliced courgettes into the batter and fry quickly in olive oil until golden. Drain and serve with roast meat or fried fish.

If smaller marrows are used, then slice them lengthwise paper thin, fry them quickly, drain and pile on a heated dish and serve immediately with *skorthalia* (see 'Sauces').

KOLOKYTHIA YIACHNI

MARROW STEW

2 lb. medium size baby marrows (courgettes)
2 or 3 onions
½ pint olive oil
1 lb. fresh ripe tomatoes
1 teaspoon chopped mint
1 teaspoon chopped fresh dill
¼ pint water
1 teaspoon sugar
Salt and pepper

Trim and scrape the marrows, leaving them whole if small enough, if not, cut them in half. Slice the onions and fry lightly in olive oil until soft but not brown. Add the sieved tomatoes and sugar to the onions and cook for ten minutes, then add the water. Season with salt and pepper. Stir well and put in the marrows and herbs. Cook gently until the marrows are tender and draw away from the fire. Stand the pan on one side for at least fifteen minutes before serving.

If liked, small new potatoes may be put in at the same time as the marrows, in which case a little extra mint should be used.

Vegetable Dishes

KOLOKYTHIA YEMISTA ME AVGOLEMONO SALTSA
STUFFED MARROWS WITH EGG AND LEMON SAUCE

2 *lb. baby marrows (courgettes)*

2 *or* 3 *onions*

½ *pint olive oil*

3 *cloves garlic*

1 *teaspoon chopped mint*

1 *tablespoon chopped dill*

1 *tablespoon chopped parsley*

6 *oz. rice*

1 *ripe tomato*

1 *teaspoon sugar*

A pinch of cinnamon

Salt and pepper

Egg and lemon sauce

Remove the pulp from the baby marrows with a potato peeler and keep on one side. Chop and fry the onion lightly in olive oil, chop the garlic and herbs and add to the onions. Add the rice and cook until it becomes pearly. Add the chopped tomato and a cupful of marrow pulp. Season with salt, pepper, sugar and cinnamon and add a little water if necessary. Cook for about fifteen minutes. Remove from the fire and when cool enough to handle, stuff the marrows, leaving room for the rice to swell. Pack them closely into a large saucepan, barely cover with water and press down with a plate. Put on the lid and simmer for one hour.

Make an egg and lemon sauce by beating two eggs with a little water until frothy. Mix in a tablespoon of cornflour and the juice of a lemon. Take two ladlefuls of stock from the pan and add slowly to the egg and lemon. Return to the pan, rock well to mix and serve without further cooking.

KOLOKYTHIA YEMISTA ME DOMATES
STUFFED MARROWS WITH TOMATOES

2 *lb. baby marrows (courgettes)*

2 *or* 3 *onions*

3 *cloves garlic*

½ *pint olive oil*

1 *dessertspoon chopped dill*

¼ *teaspoon chopped mint*

1 *tablespoon chopped parsley*

6 *oz. rice*

2 *lb. ripe tomatoes*

1 *teaspoon sugar*

Pinch of cinnamon

Salt and pepper

Remove the pulp from the marrows and put it on one side. Chop the onion and *sauté* it for a few minutes in the olive oil. Chop and add the garlic, dill, mint and parsley, then the rice and stir until the rice is pearly. Add half the sieved tomatoes and about a cupful of the marrow pulp. Season with a little salt, a grind of black pepper, a pinch of sugar and cinnamon; add a little water and cook for fifteen minutes. Remove from the fire and when cool, stuff the prepared marrows. Fry each one for a few minutes in hot olive oil, pack them in a buttered baking-dish and cover with the rest of the sieved tomatoes and cook in a moderate oven for about one hour. Care must be taken that they do not dry up in the oven. Baste from time to time and, if necessary, add more tomato juice.

KOUKIA YIACHNI   STEWED BROAD BEANS

3 *lb. young broad beans*   1 *lb. ripe tomatoes*
12 *spring onions*   ½ *pint olive oil*
1 *tablespoon dill*   1 *teaspoon sugar*
1 *teaspoon mint*   *Salt and pepper*
1 *tablespoon parsley*

If the beans are very young, leave them in the pods. Wash and trim the beans and with the chopped onions, herbs, seasoning, coarsely chopped tomatoes and olive oil put them into a large pan, stir once or twice, add a cupful of water and cook gently until the beans are tender. Draw aside from the fire and stand for half an hour before serving.

MELITZANES PAPOUTSAKIA

AUBERGINE SLIPPERS

2 *lb. aubergines (long variety)*   6 *oz. grated cheese (Parmesan or* kefalotiri)
Olive oil for frying   1 *egg*
4 *onions*   1 *pint thick Béchamel sauce (see* 'Sauces')
2 *tablespoons butter*   *Salt and pepper*

Cut the aubergines in half lengthwise. Sprinkle with salt and leave to draw the fluid for about an hour. Fry lightly in very hot olive oil and arrange them cut-side up in a baking-dish. Press the pulp down with a spoon to make a hollow in each half, season with salt and pepper and have ready the following filling:

Chop the onions and cook until soft in very little water. When half cooked add the butter and 2 tablespoons grated cheese.

Fill the hollowed aubergines with the mixture and cover each one with the Béchamel sauce into which the egg has been beaten, sprinkle the rest of the grated cheese on top and brown in the oven. Serve very hot.

Finely minced meat may be added to the filling and makes a more substantial dish.

MELITZANES STIFATHO AUBERGINE STEW

Three varieties of aubergines are grown in Greece. The round, dark, shiny kind and two long types, one being the same colour as the round kind and the other a lighter-coloured streaky purple variety.

The round fat ones are used mainly for making *melitzanes salata* or the famous *moussaka*, the others are fried, or used for such dishes as *papoutsakia* or *imam bayaldi*, for which recipes are given.

Either the long or the round variety may be used for *stifatho*.

2 *lb. aubergines*	½ *pint olive oil*
1 *lb. shallots*	2 *tablespoons wine vinegar or*
4 *cloves garlic*	*red wine*
1 *lb. ripe tomatoes*	1 *sprig sweet basil*
1 *teaspoon sugar*	1 *bay leaf*
	Pepper and salt

Cut the aubergines into pieces, sprinkle them with salt and leave them, if possible in the sun, for about an hour to drain off the rather bitter liquid. Dry them and put them into a large pan. Clean the garlic cloves and shallots, leave them whole and put them in with the aubergines. Slice the tomatoes and with the sugar, oil, wine or wine vinegar and herbs, add to the contents of the pan. Season. Simmer gently for about one hour and, if necessary, add a little water but the dish should not be watery. Draw from the fire and stand a while before serving.

MELITZANES TIGANITES   FRIED AUBERGINES

Either the long or the round variety of aubergines may be fried but whichever you use, remember to slice them and leave them to drain before cooking.

2 *lb. aubergines*	1 *egg*
Flour and water batter	*Salt and pepper*

Cut the aubergines into thin slices, sprinkle with salt and leave them, if possible in the sun, for about one hour. This will draw a green, slightly bitter fluid and leave the aubergines sweeter. Dry them with a cloth and dip each slice into a thick seasoned flour-and-water batter into which you have beaten an egg. Fry in hot olive oil until crisp and golden and serve at once.

Serve with *skorthalia* (see 'Sauces').

MOUSSAKAS HORIS KREAS
MOUSSAKA WITHOUT MEAT

4 *lb. aubergines*	*Olive oil for frying*
2 *large onions*	3 *eggs*
3 *ripe tomatoes*	1½ *pints Béchamel sauce (see*
½ *lb. grated cheese* (kefalo-tiri *or* kasseri)	'Sauces')
Butter	*Cinnamon*
	Salt and pepper

Slice two pounds of the aubergines and sprinkle with salt, leaving them to drain for about an hour. Rinse and dry them and fry lightly and quickly in olive oil and again leave them to drain.

Put the rest of the aubergines into boiling salted water or bake them in a moderate oven until soft. Chop the onion and colour lightly in butter, peel and mash the boiled aubergines, skin and chop the tomatoes and mix all together with two tablespoons of Béchamel sauce, salt, pepper and a pinch of cinnamon.

Line the bottom of a buttered baking-dish with the sliced aubergines, put in a layer of the mixture and sprinkle with grated cheese. Continue to fill the dish in layers and when nearly full, beat three eggs into the Béchamel sauce and pour over the contents of the dish. Sprinkle with cheese and bake until golden in a moderately hot oven.

PATATO-KEFTETHES   POTATO RISSOLES

6 *large potatoes*
1 *good tablespoon butter*
2 *eggs*
3 *oz. grated cheese*

3 *oz. flour*
Olive oil for frying
Salt and pepper

Peel, boil and mash the potatoes with butter. Stir in the well-beaten eggs, grated cheese and seasoning. Form into round flat cakes, not too thick. Pat firmly into the flour on a board and fry in very hot olive oil until golden. Serve at once.

PATATES YEMISTES   STUFFED POTATOES

6 *large potatoes*
3 *oz. grated cheese (Parmesan or* kefalotiri)

4 *slices bacon*
1 *pint Béchamel sauce (see* 'Sauces')

Boil the potatoes in their jackets until just cooked but still very firm. Remove the skins and hollow out some of the inside. Cut the bacon into small pieces and fry very lightly before mixing into the Béchamel sauce with half the grated cheese. Fill the hollowed potatoes with the sauce, sprinkle with the rest of the cheese and bake in a hot oven until golden.

Serve with a salad as a main dish or with roast meat.

PHROUTALIA
VEGETABLE OMELETTE (ANDROS)

1 *lb. baby marrows*
Shelled broad beans
  or
Potatoes

4 *oz. butter*
1 *teaspoon chopped mint*
6 *eggs*
Salt and pepper

Melt two ounces of butter in a frying-pan and add the sliced baby marrows, shelled broad beans or thinly sliced potatoes. Cover with a pan lid and cook slowly until any liquid from the vegetables has evaporated and the butter has been absorbed.

Put in the rest of the butter, season with salt and pepper, add the chopped mint and lastly the very well-beaten eggs. Prod the omelette all over with a fork to allow the egg to penetrate and when browned on one side, either turn out on to a plate and slip it back into the pan or finish cooking under the grill.

Phroutalia makes a delicious luncheon dish served with a mixed salad.

PRASSORIZO
LEEKS WITH RICE

6 *or* 8 *leeks*
½ *pint olive oil*
1 *dessertspoon tomato paste*
1 *teaspoon sugar*

6 *oz. rice*
Pinch of cinnamon
1 *pint water*
Salt and pepper

Cut the white part of the leeks into pieces about two inches long and put them into a saucepan without water over a low fire to draw for about ten minutes. Add the olive oil, tomato paste, sugar, cinnamon and seasoning. Stir with a wooden spoon, add the water and cook until the leeks are tender but not soft. Shower in the rice and stir well once but no more or the leeks will break up. Cook over a high flame for about five minutes. Draw away from the fire just before all the water is absorbed by the rice. Cover with a clean cloth, replace the saucepan lid and leave until the rice is fully cooked and the water completely absorbed.

Vegetable Dishes

PRASSOPITTA LEEK PIE

4 *lb. leeks*
1½ *pints Béchamel sauce (see*
   'Sauces')
2 *oz.* kefalotiri
2 *oz. Parmesan*

3 *or* 4 *eggs*
12 *oz.* filo (*pastry sheets*)
2 *oz. butter*
Salt, pepper, nutmeg

Using only the white part, boil the leeks until soft several hours, or, better still, the day before they are required. Add the grated cheese and well-beaten eggs to the sauce and, before adding the leeks, shred them with the fingers. Season to taste. Line a shallow baking-tin with five or six pastry sheets, oiling each one with melted butter as they are smoothed one on another. Spread the filling evenly and cover with the remaining well-buttered pastry sheets. Fold in the edges to seal in the filling and score the top sheets with a sharp knife. Cover with greaseproof paper and bake in a moderate oven until golden and crisp. About an hour.

SPANAKORIZO SPINACH WITH RICE

3 *lb. spinach*
3 *onions or a bunch of spring*
   onions
½ *pint olive oil*

1 *tablespoon chopped dill*
6 *oz. rice*
1 *pint water*
Salt and pepper

Put the olive oil into a large saucepan. Chop the onions coarsely and *sauté* gently until half cooked but not coloured.

Wash the spinach leaves well, removing any tough stalks and, having shaken off the surplus water, put into the saucepan with the onions. Cover and simmer gently for five minutes, then add the dill, seasoning and water and bring to the boil. Throw in the rice, stir well once with a wooden spoon and cook on a brisk fire until the rice swells and the water is reduced. When most of the water has been absorbed draw away from the fire or keep on a very low flame until the rice is cooked and the water has completely disappeared. When the

pan is drawn from the fire, a clean cloth should be placed over
the pan and the lid replaced so that the steam does not escape
altogether. Leave for ten or fifteen minutes before serving.

SPANAKOPITTA   SPINACH PIE

4 *lb. spinach*	1 *tin evaporated milk*
2 *lb. leeks*	8 *spring onions*
1 *tablespoon chopped dill or*	½ *cup olive oil*
fennel	*Butter*
1 *lb.* fetta *cheese*	*Nutmeg, salt, pepper*
5 *eggs*	1 *lb.* filo

Clean and wash the spinach thoroughly, discard the stems and
chop the leaves finely. Sprinkle with salt, squeezing and rubbing it in with the hands and leave to drain. Using only the
white part, cut the leeks into thin slices and blanch for a few
minutes in boiling water. Drain carefully and *sauté* in fresh
butter until transparent. Add the leeks to the spinach with
the sliced onions and dill, break up the *fetta* cheese with a fork
and mix well with the leeks and spinach. Next, add the beaten
eggs, milk and olive oil and season with a grind of pepper, a
grate of nutmeg and salt, if necessary.

Using half the pastry sheets, line a well-oiled baking-tin,
smoothing one on top of another, oiling each sheet. Spread the
filling evenly and cover with the remaining sheets, remembering to oil each one. Trim the edges and tuck well in to contain
the filling. Seal the edges with a little cold water and brush
the top liberally with oil. With a sharp knife score the top
two sheets into squares, cover with greaseproof paper and
bake in a moderate oven for about three-quarters of an hour
until golden and crisp on the top. Cool and cut into squares for
serving.

X

SALADS

'DIAFORA' SALATA — MIXED SALAD

Slice a Cos lettuce and a green pepper into thin strips and cut up two or three tomatoes into pieces the size of a walnut. Put them into a salad bowl with about twelve Kalamata olives and four ounces of *fetta* cheese cut into small squares. Toss in a dressing of lemon juice and olive oil seasoned with a pinch of salt and several grinds of black pepper. Variations on this salad can be made by the addition of spring onions, chopped dill or fennel, a few capers and a sliced pickled gherkin.

DOMATA SALATA — TOMATO SALAD

Slice some firm tomatoes into a shallow salad bowl with a little finely sliced onion. Sprinkle with salt and leave for ten minutes, turning once or twice. Pour a tablespoon of olive oil over the tomatoes, add a pinch of *rigani* (*oregano*) and serve. In the summer, when cucumbers and green peppers are cheap and plentiful, they are sometimes used instead of onion and a little wine vinegar is then added to the olive oil.

FASSOLIA SALATA — FRENCH BEAN SALAD

Trim and slice some French beans rather coarsely and cook them until tender in plenty of boiling salted water. Drain and leave to cool. Dress with olive oil and lemon juice or wine vinegar and serve cold with fried fish or grilled meats.

Salads

KOLOKYTHAKIA SALATA COURGETTE SALAD

Choose young courgettes about three or four inches long and still bearing the flower if fresh from the garden. Top and tail them, keeping the flowers on one side. Scrape them, if necessary, and drop into boiling salted water. Cook for about ten minutes, pour off the water and leave to drain. Leave them whole, if small enough, or cut them into chunky slices and serve with a dressing of olive oil, lemon juice, salt and a grind of black pepper.

Freshly gathered, the flowers are delicious to eat. They should be dipped into a thick seasoned batter and fried quickly in plenty of very hot olive oil.

KOUNOUPITHI SALATA CAULIFLOWER SALAD

Break a cauliflower head into manageable pieces and boil in salted water until cooked but not soft and mushy. Drain, and serve cold dressed with plenty of olive oil and lemon juice.

LACHANO SALATA SAVOY CABBAGE SALAD

Cabbages, being cheap, are the most popular of all raw winter salads in Greece. Choose one that is firm and solid and discard the outer leaves, using only the hard white part of the cabbage. Slice very finely with a sharp knife and toss in a lemon and olive oil dressing. Garnish with pomegranate seeds, capers or finely sliced onion.

MAROULI SALATA COS LETTUCE SALAD

Slice lettuce into thin strips and add some finely chopped spring onions and fresh dill. Serve with an olive oil and lemon juice or wine vinegar dressing.

PANTZARIA SALATA BEETROOT SALAD

In Greece, beetroots are gathered young and small. If they

are left in the ground too long they become tough and fibrous.

They are served boiled, sliced and dressed with an olive oil and vinegar dressing. The tops, being young and fresh, are boiled separately as they need less cooking time but are usually served together with the beetroot.

PATATES SALATA — POTATO SALAD

Choose a waxy variety of potato for making a salad. If you use the floury kind the result will be mushy and rather unappetizing.

2 *lb. small potatoes*	1 *dessertspoon wine vinegar*
1 *onion*	*Parsley*
2 *tablespoons olive oil*	*Salt and pepper*

Wash and boil the potatoes in their skins, taking care not to over-boil them or they will split. When cool enough to handle, remove the skins carefully and cut the potatoes into small cubes. Slice the onion very finely and add to the potatoes. Add a good handful of chopped parsley and while the potatoes are still warm, pour over a dressing of olive oil, wine vinegar, salt and pepper. Serve cold.

If you have some fresh dill on hand, chop up a little with the parsley. Very good with fried fish.

RADIKYA SALATA — DANDELION SALAD

Choose some young dandelion leaves and wash them well in running water. Boil them very quickly until tender in plenty of salted water, drain, and serve cold with an olive oil and lemon dressing.

This salad is delicious with cold meat, grills or fried fish and is one of the most popular salads in Greece.

SPANAKI SALATA — SPINACH SALAD

Whichever variety of spinach is used it must be picked over

leaf by leaf and the stems and tough parts removed unless very young, when they can all be cooked together. It is not really enough to wash spinach under the tap. It should be swilled round in a large bowl, changing the water several times. There are two opinions about the cooking of spinach. One way is to shake off any surplus water after rinsing and cook without the addition of more water. The Greeks, and incidentally the French, always put it into a large pan of boiling salted water and boil it rapidly for about fifteen minutes. When it is cooked, drain the spinach in a colander without pressing it too dry and when it has cooled a little, put into a serving bowl with a generous amount of olive oil and the juice of a small lemon poured over it.

VROUVA   MUSTARD OR CHARLOCK

The yellow flowering weed known as mustard which ruins a field of corn is considered to be a great delicacy in Greece and is gathered just before it flowers. Care must be taken to use only the top tender part of the stalk bearing the unopened buds. It is not at all bitter and has a very delicate flavour. Wash it well and plunge into boiling salted water. When tender, drain and serve cold with an olive oil and lemon dressing.

YAOURTI SALATA *or* TSATSIKI

YOGHOURT SALAD

Yoghourt salad is a very welcome addition to a cold buffet or summer supper party.

To one pint of yoghourt add a small cucumber, peeled and cut into tiny cubes, three cloves of finely sliced garlic or, if preferred, a few coarsely chopped mint leaves. Add salt to taste and serve very cold, garnished with a peppering of paprika.

XI

SWEETS, CAKES AND BISCUITS

Cakes made of sesame and honey, sweetmeats,
Cheese cakes and cream cakes, and a hecatomb
of new laid eggs were all devoured by us.

Athenaeus

Anyone who has seen the architectural triumphs of Athenian cake makers together with the opulent and colourful displays of pastries in Athenian shop windows must feel that the Greeks have a particular devotion to this form of creative art.

Although they have a very sweet tooth they rarely end their meals with puddings or pies but content themselves with fresh fruit which is always in plentiful supply, followed by the inevitable Turkish coffee.

Zacharoplasteia (pastry shops) abound in Athens and every village has at least one as well as a coffee-shop. It is a common practice to buy a rich cream cake, which will be served with a glass of cold water, and to eat it standing up in the shop. *Kataifi, baclavas, galatoboureko* are all Greco-Turkish sweets made from *filo*, the paper-thin pastry sheets which are professionally made and may be obtained in Greek shops everywhere.

When you visit a Greek house you will at once be offered something sweet as a welcome and, to express hospitality, a cup of Turkish coffee, a liqueur and a preserve made of orange peel, tiny unripe bitter oranges, quince or grapes or perhaps some delicious clear honey poured over shelled walnuts or almonds. These are always served on a small glass plate with a spoon and a glass of water. In fact, sweets and preserves are eaten at all times of the day but rarely after a meal.

BACLAVAS BAKLAVA

Baclavas is one of the better-known Greek sweets made with the special leaf-like pastry (*filo*), honey and nuts. It is rich and sticky and very delicious when made a day or two before it is required.

8 *oz. unsalted butter*	2 *cups chopped walnuts*
1 *cup sugar*	*Powdered cinnamon*
1 *cup water*	1 *lb.* filo

FOR THE SYRUP:

1 *cup sugar*	1 *cup water*
1 *cup honey*	*Juice of* 1 *lemon*

Heat four ounces of butter with one cup of sugar and one cup of hot water. Add the chopped nuts. Line a well-buttered baking-tin with three or four sheets of *filo*, brushing each one with melted butter. Spread a thin layer of the filling on the pastry, sprinkle with cinnamon and cover with two more sheets of buttered *filo*. Continue in this way, using alternate layers of nuts and *filo*. Tuck the ends and sides in to contain the filling. Brush the top with melted butter and score into squares or diamonds with a sharp knife. Cover the last layer of nuts with three or four sheets of *filo*, each one brushed liberally with melted butter. Bake in a moderate oven until golden and crisp.

Boil the sugar with the honey, water and lemon juice and, while still hot, pour over the *baclavas*. Leave to cool before cutting into pieces for serving.

BOUGATSA

3 *pints milk*
5 *eggs*
12 *oz. caster sugar*
6 *oz. semolina*

12 *oz.* filo (*pastry sheets*)
1 *oz. butter*
Icing sugar
Cinnamon

Scald the milk but do not let it boil. Beat the sugar and semolina into the egg yolks until white and creamy. Slowly stir in the hot milk and return to the pan, stirring all the time over a low flame until the mixture thickens. Add the butter and remove from the fire to cool. Beat the egg whites until they form peaks and fold lightly into the cooled mixture. Using half the pastry sheets, line a well-oiled shallow baking-tin, brushing each sheet with melted butter and smooth them one on top of the other. Spread the filling evenly and cover with the remaining pastry sheets, remembering to brush each sheet with melted butter. Fold in the sides and ends to prevent the filling from coming out and with the point of a very sharp knife or, better still, a razor blade, score the top two sheets into convenient sized pieces for serving. Cover with grease-proof paper and put into a hot oven. Reduce the heat and do not remove from the oven until golden brown and crisp. This will take about thirty minutes. While still hot, sprinkle the top with icing sugar and cinnamon and serve hot or cold.

CAFES

There are no more dedicated coffee drinkers than the Greeks and it must be a non-stop irritant to a proud people that their second national beverage is blanketed under the name of Turkish coffee. In the hotels you will be asked if you will have the offer of Turkish coffee or Nescafe and when you choose Nescafe you are likely to receive something else as Nescafe has paid the penalty of its success and become the international word for instant coffee.

Experts say that there are thirty-five different ways of making Turkish coffee. The three main kinds are *glikos*, meaning sweet; *metrios*, which is made with half sugar and half coffee, and *schetos*, made without any sugar at all. These three form the basis for all the variations and it is simply a question of more or less sugar, how long the coffee should be boiled, how many times removed from the fire and put back, how often it should be stirred and whether there should be a froth or not.

A special long-handled, lipped, copper or aluminium pot known as a *briki* is used which holds just the right amount of water and coffee. *Brikia* are made in several sizes for one, two, four or six cups of coffee and can be bought in many coffee shops dealing exclusively with coffee and tea.

To make Turkish coffee without a *briki*, put one heaped teaspoon of sugar and one flat teaspoon of Turkish coffee to each small coffee cup of cold water into a small saucepan and bring to the boil. Remove from the flame and stir once. Return to the flame and boil once more. Pour into the coffee cups and serve with a glass of cold water. The coffee must be freshly ground and specially fine. Ask for Turkish grind.

DIPLES
PASTRY BOWS

For generations these have been the Greek child's favourite just as pancakes have been the favourite of the British child.

2 *cups flour*	4 *eggs*
1 *teaspoon baking powder*	*Grated rind of* 1 *small orange*
5 *tablespoons olive oil*	½ *teaspoon salt*

Sift the flour twice with the baking powder and salt and mix with the olive oil. Add the well-beaten eggs and the orange rind and knead to a soft dough. Leave to stand in the refrigerator for half an hour or more. Roll out to a paper thinness and, with a pastry wheel, cut into long strips about one inch wide. Carefully tie into bows and fry them in deep boiling oil until golden. Dry on a sheet of greaseproof paper and pile them on to a serving dish. Pour some warm honey over them and sprinkle them generously with powdered cinnamon and chopped walnuts.

FILO

Filo is a leaf-like form of pastry and is used for many sweet, cheese and savoury dishes. It is rarely made at home nowadays except in the country and is obtainable in Greek food shops in London and any big city where there is a Greek or Cypriot community.

Filo made at home can never be stretched as thinly as the bought variety and in recipes where several sheets or layers are called for, fewer thickness will be required.

12 oz. flour	Pinch of salt
1 dessertspoon olive oil	Water

Sieve the flour and salt together, add the oil and as much water as is required to make a firm dough. Knead well and roll out as thinly as possible on a floured cloth and with the hands, stretch gently and carefully until the dough is stretched to the thinness of paper. Leave for three-quarters of an hour to dry and use as required.

GALATOBOUREKO

1 lb. filo	4 oz. butter
2 pints milk	6 eggs
6 oz. sugar	1 teaspoon vanilla essence
6 oz. fine semolina	Pinch of salt

FOR THE SYRUP:

12 oz. sugar	1 dessertspoon lemon juice
1½ cups water	Lemon peel

Heat the milk to boiling point with the sugar, semolina, two ounces of butter, vanilla essence, a good pinch of salt and a sliver of lemon peel. Stir constantly until the mixture thickens smoothly and is free from lumps. Boil for a few minutes, then remove from the fire and continue to stir to keep the mixture smooth and to prevent the formation of a crust while cooling. Beat the eggs well and stir into the contents of the pan when cooled sufficiently.

Line a buttered baking-tin with half the sheets of the pastry, lapping them over the edge of the tin. Brush each sheet with melted butter as they are smoothed one on top of the other. Spread the filling evenly with a spatula. Cover with the remaining pastry sheets, remembering to butter each one. Trim the edges and fold in carefully so that the filling is well contained. Brush the top with melted butter and seal the edges with a little cold water. Score the top sheets with a sharply pointed knife or, better still, a razor blade, diagonally across the pan about three inches wide and bake in a moderate oven for about three-quarters of an hour until golden.

Meanwhile boil the sugar, water, lemon juice and a sliver of lemon peel about ten minutes until the syrup thickens.

When the *galatoboureko* is ready and still hot from the oven, spoon the syrup over it a little at a time until absorbed by the pastry. Leave to cool and cut into diamond shapes before serving.

This sweet is better if it is made a day before it is required as the filling should be firm and the *filo* soaked with the syrup.

HALVAS TIS RENAS
HALVA

8 *oz. fine semolina*	4 *oz. butter*
4 *oz. ground almonds*	4 *eggs*
8 *oz. sugar*	1 *teaspoon ground cinnamon*

FOR THE SYRUP:

6 *oz. sugar*	*Juice of* 1 *lemon*
1 *cup water*	

Beat the butter with the sugar until white and fluffy and add the beaten eggs, cinnamon, ground almonds and semolina. Pour into a well-greased baking-tin and cook in a moderate oven for one hour. When cooked but still warm, make a syrup with the sugar, water and lemon juice and boil until it begins to thicken. Remove from the fire and cool slightly before pouring over the halva.

KATAIFI

Probably together with *baclava* the best-known Greek sweet. Like *filo*, the leaf-like pastry used in making *baclavas*, *kataifi* is bought by the kilo and is to be found in the same shops selling *filo*. To watch *kataifi* being made is a fascinating experience.

A batter of flour and water is poured into a hopper which feeds a fine stream on to a very hot rotating turntable in ever-widening circles, from which the operator scoops up loops of the thread-like *kataifi* with his hand at just the right moment before it becomes overcooked and brittle.

When ready to eat, *kataifi* looks very like shredded wheat, which can in fact be used when fresh *kataifi* is unobtainable.

1 *lb.* kataifi	4 *oz. unsalted butter*
1 *cup chopped walnuts and almonds*	3 *oz. sugar*
	1 *teaspoon cinnamon*

FOR THE SYRUP:

8 *oz. sugar*	½ *cup honey*
1 *cup water*	*Juice of* 1 *lemon*

If fresh *kataifi* is used, line a greased baking-tin with half the *kataifi*. Melt the butter and mix with the sugar, chopped nuts and cinnamon. Spread the mixture in the tin and cover with the rest of the *kataifi*. Mark the top into squares and bake in a moderate oven until golden.

For the syrup, heat the sugar, water, honey and lemon juice together to boiling point. Allow to cool a little and pour over the *kataifi*. When it is well soaked in syrup, cut into squares for serving.

Another method is to form rolls of the *kataifi* stuffed with the filling before baking, but this method needs a good deal of practice.

If fresh *kataifi* is not available and shredded wheat is used, allow 2 rolls for each person. Dip the shredded wheat in milk and place them side by side in the baking-tin. Spread with the filling and cover with another layer of rolls. Heat in the oven for fifteen minutes, pour the hot syrup on top and cool before serving.

KOULOURAKIA

12 oz. butter	1 tablespoon cooking brandy
1 cup sugar	1 teaspoon baking soda
½ cup warm water	½ teaspoon vanilla essence
Salt	Flour

Cream the butter and sugar together for five minutes. Dissolve the baking soda in the warm water and beat into the creamed butter and sugar with the brandy, vanilla essence and a pinch of salt. Sieve and mix as much flour as the mixture will take to make a dough firm enough to handle. Tear off pieces of the dough and roll between the hands and on a pastryboard to form thin rolls about nine inches long. Turn both ends back on each other to make three thicknesses and pinch together before placing them on a greased baking-sheet. Brush each one with a little beaten egg and bake in a moderate oven for fifteen minutes.

KOURABIEDES

8 oz. butter	Rose water
4 oz. caster sugar	1 dessertspoon brandy
1 lb. flour	½ teaspoon baking soda
4 oz. ground almonds	Pinch of salt
Yolk of 1 egg	4 oz. icing sugar

Beat the butter together with four ounces of sugar until white and creamy. Add the brandy and well-beaten egg yolk, followed by the sieved flour, baking soda, pinch of salt and ground almonds. Knead well for a few minutes and form into balls about the size of an egg. Flatten slightly on to a greased baking-sheet and bake in a cool oven for twenty minutes until firm and crisp but not browned. While still warm from the oven, sprinkle each one with a little rose water and dredge very liberally with the icing sugar. Serve piled into a mound on a cake plate.

LATHERO KEIK OIL CAKE

1 *cup olive oil*	*Juice and rind of* 1 *orange and*
12 *oz. sugar*	*tangerine or lemon*
1½ *lb. flour*	1 *tablespoon brandy*
12 *oz. currants*	1 *level teaspoon baking soda*
Salt	*Salt and cinnamon*

Beat the oil and sugar together. Sift the baking soda and cinnamon with the flour and salt and add to the oil and sugar alternately with the juice of the orange and tangerine. Roll the currants in a little flour so that they will not fall to the bottom of the cake and add to the mixture with the grated rinds of orange and tangerine. Lastly add the brandy. If the dough seems too stiff, add a little water.

Pour into a well-greased baking-tin and cook in a moderate oven for about one hour. To serve, cut into squares. This cake keeps well.

LOUCOUMADES HONEY PUFFS

There are special pastry shops in Athens which serve only *loucoumades*. Made while you wait, they are always served with a glass of ice-cold water. They are not difficult to make at home provided the yeast is given time to work. They should be light and fluffy, powdered with cinnamon and dripping with honey.

8 *oz. flour*	½ *teaspoon salt*
2 *oz. yeast*	*Powdered cinnamon*
½ *pint warm water*	*Oil for frying*

FOR THE SYRUP:

1 *cup honey*	*Juice of* 1 *lemon*
½ *cup water*	

Dissolve the yeast in a basin with some warm water. Add two tablespoons of flour and leave to rise in a warm place for half an hour. When the yeast has worked, add the rest of the flour and enough warm water to make a thick batter of dropping consistency. Cover the basin with a cloth and let it stand for two or three hours until bubbles appear on the top. The batter is then ready for frying.

Put at least one pint of olive oil into a deep pan and when really hot drop the batter from a spoon, dipping the spoon into cold water each time before dipping into the batter, thus the batter will not stick to the spoon. Cook until golden. Dry on a sheet of greaseproof paper and pile on a warmed plate for serving. Dust with cinnamon and pour on the warm syrup. Serve at once.

MELOMACARONA (FINIKIA)

PHOENICIAN HONEY CAKES

Finika is another name for the small honey cakes offered to callers at a Greek home at Christmas and New Year. The recipe is said to have been brought to Greece by the Phoenicians who are also said to have introduced the Greek alphabet.

Some people use semolina, but one of the best Greek cooks I know makes her *melomacarona* with flour only and having tasted both, I prefer them made with flour.

2 *lb. flour (approx.)*	1 *liqueur glass brandy*
2 *cups olive oil*	1 *teaspoon cinnamon*
½ *cup sugar*	½ *teaspoon ground cloves*
½ *cup retsina (white wine)*	½ *teaspoon ground nutmeg*
½ *cup orange juice*	*Salt*

FOR THE SYRUP:

2 *cups honey*	1 *cup cold water*
1 *cup sugar*	1 *lemon*

Sieve the flour and work little by little into the oil and other ingredients until a fairly stiff dough is achieved, adding more liquid if too stiff and more flour if too soft to handle. Knead well for about fifteen minutes. Pinch off a piece at a time and form into balls the size and shape of an egg, flattening them lightly on an oiled baking-sheet and bake in a hot oven for fifteen minutes until brown. Meanwhile, make a syrup of the sugar, honey, water and lemon juice and boil until it is frothy.

When the *melomacarona* are ready, take from the oven and while still warm lower each one into the hot syrup for two or three minutes and place on a sheet of greaseproof paper to cool. Sprinkle with chopped almonds and a powdering of cinnamon.

RIZOGALO   GREEK RICE PUDDING

1½ *pints milk*   1 *egg yolk*
2 *tablespoons sugar*   *Cinnamon*
1½ *tablespoons rice*   *Pinch of salt*
Lemon peel

Boil the milk, sugar and rice together with a piece of lemon peel, preferably in a double saucepan. Add a pinch of salt and cook very slowly until the rice has absorbed all the milk. Remove from the fire and cool a little before mixing in the egg yolk beaten up in a little cold milk. Cook for a few minutes longer and pour on to individual plates. When cold, sprinkle generously with cinnamon.

SAVOYARD

8 *oz. Savoy biscuits*   *Rum or cognac*
8 *oz. unsalted butter*   *Toasted almonds*
1 *cup icing sugar*   *Milk*
Chocolate powder or powdered coffee

Dip the Savoy biscuits in a little rum or cognac and milk to soften. Let them soak up some of the liquid but do not leave too long or they will become soggy. Arrange them packed closely together on a serving plate, trimming them into shape.

Meanwhile, cream the butter and sugar and beat until fluffy and add enough chocolate powder or powdered coffee to give colour and flavour with a little more rum or cognac. Spread a layer of the butter mixture over the Savoy biscuits. Arrange another layer of biscuits and smooth the rest of the creamed butter over the top and round the sides. Decorate with chopped toasted almonds and place in the refrigerator for at least one hour before serving.

SIPHNOPITTA   SIPHNOS PIE

This is a special Easter sweet made on the island of Siphnos. It is made with the Greek cheese *mizithra*, an unsalted soft cheese made from ewe's milk. In England a fresh cottage cheese may be substituted.

1 *lb.* mizithra *or cottage cheese*	8 *oz. butter*
8 *oz. honey*	4 *eggs*
4 *oz. sugar*	*Salt*
8 *oz. flour*	*Cinnamon*

Mix the cheese, sugar and honey together in a bowl. Beat the eggs well and add to the cheese mixture and work thoroughly.

Prepare a flaky pastry with the flour, butter, a little salt and water. Line a greased baking-tin with the pastry and spread with the filling. Bake in a moderate oven for thirty or thirty-five minutes until golden brown. Dust the top well with cinnamon. Cool and cut into squares for serving.

SVINGI   BEIGNETS

1 *cup water*	1 *cup flour*
½ *oz. butter*	1 *teaspoon baking soda*
½ *teaspoon salt*	2 *or* 3 *eggs*

Heat the water with the butter and salt and just before boiling point is reached, add the flour and baking soda and stir vigorously until the paste leaves the sides of the pan.

Draw away from the fire and rest for a few minutes. Break the eggs one by one and work into the *roux*. When the eggs are absorbed, beat vigorously for fifteen minutes. Leave to rest for two to three hours before cooking. The secret of making *svingi* lies in the old advice about dogs, women and the walnut tree, 'the more they are beaten the better they be'.

Have ready a deep pan of olive oil, at least one pint, and when very hot but not smoking, take a teaspoonful of the *roux* and drop into the pan one at a time. When the *svingi* break the surface of the oil turn them over and cook until golden.

The *svingi* should be very light and puffy like ping-pong balls and should be served hot with warmed honey and cinnamon or, if preferred, a syrup of sugar and water.

TIGANITES FRITTERS

3 *heaped tablespoons flour*　　*Pinch of salt*
1 *cup water*　　　　　　　　*Olive oil for frying*
¼ *teaspoon baking soda*

Sieve the flour, baking soda and salt together and mix with water to a rather stiff dropping consistency. Using a wooden spoon, beat the batter well until smooth and creamy and leave to stand for half an hour. Have ready a pint of very hot olive oil in a frying-pan and drop in one dessertspoonful of the batter at a time. Fry quickly on both sides until golden. Pile the fritters on a dish and pour over them some warmed honey, sprinkle with cinnamon and sugar and serve at once.

TSOUREKI EASTER BREAD

Of all the feast days celebrated in Greece, Easter is the most important and involves as much preparation in the kitchen as Christmas does for the northern European housewife. Dozens of eggs must be dyed red and polished with olive oil, the Paschal Lamb prepared for the spit and the *tsoureki* made.

Sweets, Cakes and Biscuits

Although bakery shop windows are a gay and appetizing sight during Easter Week when they are filled with many different shapes and sizes of *tsourekia*, all decorated with red eggs, many housewives still feel compelled to make the traditional *tsoureki* at home.

3 *lb. flour*	5 *eggs*
2 *oz. yeast*	1 *teaspoon caraway seeds*
1 *cup milk*	*Sugar*
4 *oz. butter*	2 *tablespoons brandy*

The secret of a good *tsoureki* is to prepare it in a constant and warm atmosphere, free from draughts and changing temperature.

First put the yeast in a bowl and soften with a little warm water. Add one cup of warm milk and mix to a creamy consistency with one and a half cups of flour. Cover and leave to rise for one hour.

Sieve the remainder of the flour into a large mixing bowl and make a hole in the middle of the flour. When the yeast has risen, pour it into the hole and flick in some of the flour from the sides. Add the well-beaten eggs, sugar, caraway seeds and brandy and knead in the flour until the dough begins to leave the sides of the bowl. Melt the butter and knead into the dough until it becomes elastic. Form into a large ball and leave to rise in a warm place covered with a cloth and, if necessary, a blanket. I have even seen a carpet whipped from the floor and tucked round the bowl for extra warmth. Leave the dough to rise for about three hours, or overnight, if you prefer to bake in the morning.

When well risen, tear off pieces of dough and roll out thickly on a floured baking board. Shape into braids, large or small, or, if preferred, place in a round shallow cake tin, cover and leave to rise once more. Decorate with split almonds, brush with white of egg and press in one or more red eggs. Bake in a moderate oven about one hour.

VASSILOPITTA

The ceremony of cutting the cake goes back to the days of Byzantium and traditionally takes place after returning home from Church on New Year's Eve or on the morning of New Year's Day, when the family is assembled together.

The head of the family performs the ceremony with his family gathered about him. The first piece he cuts is for Christ and placed on one side, the second piece is for the house, the third for the head of the house, usually the father, the fourth is for the mother and each succeeding piece is cut for other members of the family in order of age, boys taking precedence over girls, until the cake has been divided equally.

Traditionally, a golden coin is baked in the cake but nowadays only the rich can afford this and most people have to be content with a nickel drachma. Whoever finds the coin in his or her portion will have good luck in the coming year. If, however, the coin is found to be in the portion laid aside for Christ then it is either given to the Church or to someone in great need, the decision being left to the head of the house.

Some cooks use the same recipe for *tsourekia* and *vassilopitta* although most prefer to use a different one. The following makes a delicious bread with a subtle difference in texture and flavour from the *tsoureki* recipe given. It is equally necessary to work in an even temperature.

2 *lb. flour*	5 *eggs*
½ *lb. butter*	2 *oz. yeast*
2 *cups sugar*	1 *teaspoon salt*
1 *cup milk*	*Sesame seed*

Break up the yeast and mix with the previously warmed milk, add a handful of flour, cover, and leave to work. Make a hole in the sieved flour and salt, break in the eggs one by one and add the melted butter, sugar, yeast and milk. Drawing in the flour little by little, knead thoroughly for twenty minutes. If the dough is too solid, add more warm milk. Cover with a floured cloth and leave to rise for at least three hours in a warm room

free from draughts. The coin should be inserted while knead-
ing the dough.

When fully risen, knead gently for five minutes, then put the
dough into a round baking-tin called a *tapsi*, or a large shallow
cake tin will do. Cover once more and leave to rise. Brush the
top with the white of egg and scatter with sesame seed.

Bake in a moderate oven for one hour or until brown and
resilient to the touch.

YAOURTI   YOGHOURT

Throughout the Balkans and Middle East *yaourti* or *yoghourt* is served as a sweet, a sauce or a salad (see page 130). As
a sauce, it is served plain with a *pilafe*. It is eaten for breakfast
with sugar or honey and makes a delicious and refreshing
sweet if one pint of thick *yaourti* is beaten until smooth with
two or three tablespoons of caster sugar and the rind of one
orange or lemon. Thin down to the consistency of thick cream
with orange or lemon juice and serve ice-cold.

YAOURTOPITTA   YOGHOURT CAKE

4 *oz. butter*	3 *cups flour*
3 *cups sugar*	1 *lemon*
6 *eggs*	1 *tablespoon baking soda*
1 *cup yoghourt*	*Salt*

Beat the butter and sugar with the hand and add the beaten
egg yolks and yoghourt. Sieve the flour with the baking soda
and a pinch of salt and add slowly to the mixture with the juice
and grated rind of the lemon.

Beat the egg whites until they form peaks and fold into the
mixture with a knife. Pour into a greased and floured cake ring
and bake in a moderate oven for one hour. Turn out on to a
cake rack to cool and dust with icing sugar.

LIST OF SHOPS

Below is a list of London shops keeping comprehensive stocks of Greek groceries.

THE ATHENIAN GROCERY,   BAY 6280
    16a Moscow Road, London W.2.

EAST AND WEST STORES,   BAY 6336
    119 Westbourne Grove, London W.2.

HELLENIC PROVISION STORES LTD.,   MUSEUM 4406
    25 Charlotte Street, London W.1.

JOHN AND PASCALIS LTD.,   EUSTON 8182
    35 Grafton Way, London W.1.

MRS. OLIVE HARAL,
    Inverness Street, London N.W.1

GREEN ISLAND STORES,
    Delancey Street, London N.W.1

F. RICHARDS JUNR. LTD.,   GERRARD 1358
    Fishmongers (Octopus, Squid, etc., when available),
    11 Brewer Street, London W.1.

COMMONWEALTH BUTCHERS,   EUSTON 6383
    265 Eversholt Street, London N.W.1.

GLOSSARY OF TERMS

Alati	Salt	*Fresca*	Fresh
Alevri	Flour	*Gala*	Milk
Amygdala	Almonds	*Garithes*	Prawns
Anginares	Artichokes	*Khirino*	Pork
Angouri	Cucumber	*Kimas*	Minced meat
Anitho	Dill	*Kimino*	Cumin
Arakas	Peas	*Kithonia*	Quince
Arni	Lamb	*Kolokythia*	Courgette or
Astakos	Lobster		baby marrow
Avgo	Egg	*Kotopoulo*	Chicken
Avgolemono	Egg and	*Kounoupithi*	Cauliflower
	Lemon	*Krassi*	Wine
Bamyes	Okra or	*Kreas*	Meat
	ladies' fingers	*Koukia*	Broad beans
Brisola	Chop	*Lachano*	Cabbage
Chamomile	Chamomile	*Lathi*	Oil
Canella	Cinnamon	*Latholemono*	Oil and lemon
Capari	Capers	*Lathoxitho*	Oil and
Daphni	Bay		vinegar
Dendrolivano	Rosemary	*Lemoni*	Lemon
Domates	Tomatoes	*Maidano*	Parsley
Elies	Olives	*Marouli*	Cos Lettuce
Fakki	Brown lentils	*Melitzanes*	Aubergines
Fava	Yellow lentils	*Moschari*	Veal
Fassolia	Beans	*Nero*	Water
Fournos	Oven	*Octapothi*	Octopus

Glossary of Terms

Paithakia	Cutlets	*Sikoti*	Liver
Pantzaria	Beetroot	*Soupa*	Soup
Patates	Potatoes	*Spanaki*	Spinach
Piperi	Pepper	*Tiganita*	Fried
Piperies	Green	*Tilio*	Lime flowers
	peppers	*Tiri*	Cheese
Psari	Fish	*Thiosmos*	Mint
Psito	Roast	*Thymari*	Thyme
Psomi	Bread	*Xera*	Dried
Revythia	Chick peas	*Xithi*	Vinegar
Rigani	Origano	*Yaourti*	Yoghourt
Rizi	Rice	*Yemista*	Stuffed
Salata	Salad	*Vassilikos*	Sweet basil
Saltsa	Sauce	*Vrasto*	Boiled
Selino	Celery	*Vutiro*	Butter
Skara	Grill	*Zachari*	Sugar
Skortho	Garlic		

REFERENCES

G. B. GULICK: *Life of the Ancient Greeks.*

T. R. GLOVER: *Challenge of the Greek.*

N. TSELEMENDES: *Greek Cookery.*

C. D. Yonge (Trans.): *Banquet of the Learned or The Deipnosophists Athenaeus.*

CARY and HAARHOFF: *Life and Thought in the Greek and Roman World.*

T. G. TUCKER: *Life in Ancient Athens.*

SANDERS: *Encyclopaedia of Gardening.*

XEN. MESSINESI: *Meet the Ancient Greeks.*

INDEX

Achinoi (sea urchins), 67
Alcibiades, 16
Almond cakes, 138
Anginares ala polita (artichokes in oil), 109
Anginares me koukia (artichokes with broad beans), 108
Anitho (dill), 29
Appetizers hors d'oeuvre, 34–42
Archestratus (writer on cooking), 21
Arni exochico (lamb cooked in paper), 80
Arni fricassé (lamb fricassé), 81
Arni kapama (lamb ragoût), 81
Arni psito (roast lamb), 82
Arni sto lathoharto (lamb cooked in paper), 83
Artichokes (globe), 107, 108; in oil, 109; with broad beans, 108; moussaka with, 92
Asparagus, wild, 107
Astakos (crawfish, spiny lobster), 67
Athenaeus, author of *The Deipnosophists*, 17; quoted, 29, 34, 43, 55, 66, 79, 100, 106
Athens and the Greek Miracle (C. P. Rodocanachi), 15
Aubergines, 108; baked with minced meat and béchamel

sauce, 91; fried, 122; papoutsakia, 120; pickle, 37; salad, 35, 37, 38; stew, 121; stuffed, 113
Avli (courtyard), 27
Avgolemono saltsa (egg and lemon sauce), 44
Avgolemono soupa (egg and lemon soup), 56

Baccalyaros me skorthalia (salt cod with garlic sauce), 68
Baclavas (baklava), 132
Bamyes (stewed ladies' fingers), 110
Barbouni (red mullet), 68
Basil, 33
Bay, 30; bay-leaf water in laundering, 31
Bean and tomato stew, 112
Beans: broad, with artichokes, 108; broad, stewed, 120; runner, 108; *see also* Fassolia me kreas *and* Fassolia salata
Becatsa me krassi (woodcock with wine), 101
Becatses (French woodcock), 100
Béchamel sauce, origin of, 43; Béchamel saltsa (white sauce), 44

151

Index

Beetroot, 107
Beignets (svingi), 142
Birds of Greece, 100
Biscuits (koulourakia), 138
Bougatsa (custard pie), 133
Bouillabaisse, origin of, 55
Bows (diples: fried pastry bows), 134
Bourekakia (small savoury pasties), 35
Bourtheto (Corfu baked fish), 69
Bread, Easter (tsoureki), 143
Briki (coffee pot), 134
Broad beans, stewed (koukia yiachni), 120
Brown lentil soup, 57

Cabbage leaves, stuffed (dolmathes), 83
Cafes (coffee), 133-4
Cakes: almond, 138; New Year, 145; oil, 139; Phoenician honey, 140; yoghourt, 146
Capers (capari), 29
Celery, 32
Chamomile, 30
Charlock (mustard), 107
Cheese: fried, 39, 41; pastries, 42; pie, 51; puffs, 41; *fetta*, 35, 40, 41, 42 (and in various recipes); goats' milk, 20, 41; *kasseri*, 39, 41; *kefalotiri*, 39, 41; *mizithra*, 142
Chef's cap, origin of, 17
Chestnut turkey stuffing, 101
Chick pea soup, 64
Chicken, Greek treatments of, 103; pie, 51; soup, 61; stuffed, 103
Coffee, 133-4
Cos lettuce, 106, 107
Courgettes, 114; fried, 118; stuffed flowers, 115
Crawfish, 71-2

Cumin, 31
Cuttlefish, 71-2

Dandelion leaves, 107; in salad, 129
Daphni (bay), 30
Deipnosophists, see Athenaeus
Dendrolivano (rosemary), 30
'Diafora' salata (mixed salad), 127
Dill, 29
Diples (pastry bows), 134
Dolmathakia (small stuffed vine leaves), 35
Dolmathes (stuffed vine or cabbage leaves), 83; Crisulla's recipe (meatless), 110
Domata salata (tomato salad), 127
Domata saltsa (tomato sauce), 44
Domata saltsa me kima (tomato sauce with minced veal), 45
Domates me mayonaisa (tomatoes with mayonnaise), 111
Domates yemistes (tomatoes stuffed with meat), 84
Domates yemistes horis kreas (stuffed tomatoes), 112
Domatosoupa (tomato soup), 56
Dressing: olive oil and lemon, 46; olive oil and vinegar, 46
Duck, wild, 100

Easter: bread, 143; ceremonies, 61-2, 80, 142-3; soup (mayeritsa), 80; recipe for, 61
Egg and lemon soup, 56
Eggs, dyed, for Easter, 143

Fakki (brown lentil soup), 57
Faskomilo (sage), 31
Fassolatha (haricot bean soup), 57; as staple winter dish, 55

152

Index

Index

Index

Index

Index